It's the Berries!

Exotic and Common Recipes

by
Liz Anton and Beth Dooley

A Garden Way Publishing Book

Storey Communications, Inc.
Schoolhouse Road
Pownal, VT 05261

*We dedicate this book to our
families—past, present, and
future 'cause—they're the berries!*

Front cover art by Wanda Harper

Typesetting by Jackson Typesetting Co.
Designed and produced by Wanda Harper
Edited by Constance L. Oxley
© **Copyright 1988 by Storey Communications, Inc.**

The name Garden Way Publishing is licensed to Storey Communications, Inc. by Garden Way, Inc.

Printed in the United States by Hamilton Printing Company
First printing, November 1987

Library of Congress Cataloging-in-Publication Data
Anton, Liz.
    It's the berries!
    "A Garden Way Publishing book."
    Bibliography: p. 151
    Includes index.
    1. Cookery (Berries)   I. Dooley, Beth.   II. Title.
TX813. B4A58   1988   641.6'47   87-45580
ISBN 0-88266-424-7
ISBN 0-88266-425-5 (pbk.)

Contents

Introduction

*S*weet summer berries kindle memories of twilight suppers on the screened porch, the sound of crickets chirping, and the smell of freshly mowed grass.

July was spent by our family in the Pocono Mountains of eastern Pennsylvania where tiny, heavily seeded strawberries grew alongside daisies, and robust raspberries hid low near hiking trails. Liz, my mother, and I have shared bug-bitten hours of blueberry picking to earn Sunday's long awaited reward—blueberry pie with vanilla ice cream. (Who doesn't share such innocent lust?) Those sweet afternoons, even the pie stains were forgiven with an indulgent, "Oh, that will come out with bleach."

Each Christmas (in family tradition) cranberries are tossed into muffins, breads, and compotes with holiday abandon. My grandmother's recipe for zesty orange-cranberry relish is served in her cut crystal bowl. Placed in the center of the table on her mother's lace cloth, this Christmas dish shines ruby brilliant recalling memories of her kitchen. Here, we chopped the cranberries in a heavy grinder fastened to the counter with a thumbscrew, and later, cut tiny sugar cookies with thimbles for Santa's elves. For days we strung popcorn and cranberries for the Christmas tree—a ritual we continue each year.

The memories of putting up elderberry jelly are as vivid for Liz as the deep purple mash bubbling down on the back of the stove. Poured into a cheesecloth cone that hung from the ceiling it dripped for days, leaving lavender splash stains, later removed with bleach.

When the jelly jars were finally sealed with paraffin wax, Liz and her friends took the discarded scraps, coated with jam, to chew. It was as sweet as bubble gum.

Vermont vacations taught us how to scout lowbush blueberries and huckleberries on cool mountain tops. That memory was recalled this summer in Montana, where I shared the secret huckleberry patch of a close friend. Tucked in the foothills above Flathead Lake, these lush thickets are "huckle heaven," known only to the natives of Lakeville and the bears.

On the same trip, my friend's three-year old daughter, having eaten her fill of rich sweet raspberries that grew just outside the cabin, attempted to fill her pockets and I knew just how she felt as we dashed to catch the plane home.

Liz now lives in New Jersey, and I'm in Minnesota—both areas well within reach of the country's best berry growing. We've enjoyed the Blueberry Festival in Somerville, New Jersey and Raspberry Day in Hopkins, Minnesota. From Coos Bay, Oregon to Cape Cod, Massachusetts, we've collected recipes and local stories. Our work helps close the geographic distance between us—a fact that does not soften with years.

Like the berry lovers we've met in our travels, we share a passion for those fleeting moments when sunwarmed fruit is at its fragrant best and life itself is the berries.

Information on selection, storage, handling, freezing, seasonality, and growing, as well as berry history, cooking tips, and bits of kitchen lore are all here for easy reference and fun.

There also is included a chart on berries, a description of the berries, and some tips on purchasing and storing berries.

We selected the recipes for reasons as varied as the berries themselves. Separately, and together we've searched family recipes scratched on the back of envelopes; we've poured over

cracked yellowed newspaper and magazine clips. We wanted to offer the best traditional dishes, the latest creations, and old-time favorites.

The Different Berries

A berry is a fleshy fruit that doesn't split open, has many seeds (but no stone, like a cherry), and develops from one large ovary.

Blackberries. (includes the following five varieties) Purple-black with a deep wine flavor, blackberries add flavor to chicken and game, make delicious pies, tarts, jellies, and jams. Best suited to temperate climates; some varieties will grow as far north as Alaska, as far south as Florida. Blackberries do not like sandy soil, preferring moist areas with good drainage.

Blackberries are not ripe when they first turn black. They must be harvested when they are sweet and ready to drop off the bush at the slightest touch. Most varieties bear fruit in mid- to late summer. Blackberries are a good source of vitamins A and B.

Blueberries. Lowbush or wild blueberries are those tiny sweet berries enjoyed by hikers and mountain climbers. Highbush blueberries, larger and sturdier berries, are those cultivated for commercial use.

Highbush blueberries do best in the eastern United States and prefer sandy soil. They should be allowed to hang on plants for at least one week after turning blue. Ripe blueberries will come loose easily and drop off into the hand. Blueberries are in season mid- to late summer.

Blueberries may be stored a bit longer than most summer berries. They will last almost a week in the refrigerator if placed

in dry, tightly covered glass jars. Blueberries are a good source of vitamins A and C, potassium, and calcium.

Boysenberries. Larger and longer than blackberries (about 1¼ by 1 inch thick), boysenberries are dark reddish black when fully ripe, slightly acidic, and somewhat seedy.

Cranberries. A close cousin of the blueberry, cranberries are so full of vitamin C, early American explorers carried them on board ship to prevent scurvy. Cranberries grow in bogs in acidic, sandy soil and are harvested in late fall.

Currants. Currants have never been as popular among Americans as among the British, who have cultivated black, red, and white currants for canning, preserving, and eating fresh. Currants are relatively easy to grow except in very hot, dry regions. They bloom in the spring and bear fruit in mid-summer.

Dewberries. Blue-gray and a bit more delicate in flavor than blackberries, dewberries are trailing, ground-running berries and are generally grown in warmer climates. They ripen earlier than blackberries, shortly after raspberries.

Elderberries. This small, black, tart, and hard berry is known as the "magic berry" because of its medicinal properties. Elderberries are best suited to jelly, pies, and breads (as well as wine).

Elderberries grow in all but the very coldest areas. They bear fruit in early summer. Elderberries are very high in vitamin C.

Gooseberries. A truly British berry, gooseberries have never really caught on in the States. The green gooseberry has a sharp flavor and is best suited to pies and tarts. Other types of gooseberries include white, yellow, and red, which are grown to be eaten out of hand and for dessert dishes.

Huckleberries. Huckleberries are an American legend, thanks to Mark Twain. Huckleberries resemble small blueberries, are a deep blue-purple, and have a rich, tart-sweet distinctive flavor. They make excellent pies, jellies, and jams, and are delicious eaten fresh with enough sugar.

Huckleberry patch locations are well-guarded secrets passed down through generations in Montana and other western states. In the Flathead Lake region of Montana, only the natives know the whereabouts of "Huckle Heaven." Their season is mid- to late summer.

Kiwifruit. The kiwifruit is really a Chinese gooseberry renamed for the tiny fuzzy bird by New Zealand traders who introduced the fruit to California ports.

Kiwifruit is now being cultivated in California. It stores exceptionally well, and will keep up to six weeks in the refrigerator. The skin should should be peeled away (although it is edible). It should feel soft as a ripe pear for best eating. The kiwifruit is a very rich source of vitamin C. Like pineapple, kiwifruit has the curious property of tenderizing meat.

Loganberries. Loganberries have a blackberry shape and a raspberry color. They are better suited than either the blackberry or raspberry for cooking and making wonderful jam.

Mulberries. Mulberry trees are not cultivated for commercial use in America. The sweetly distinctive fruit, delicious when fresh in baked goods or in jam, is too perishable to ship. It will not keep more than one day. Mulberry trees will grow almost anywhere except in extremely hot or cold climates. Different varieties bear fruit throughout the summer.

Olallieberries. Deep black and firm, olallieberries are a cross

between the black logan and the blackberry. They are tender and seedy.

Raspberries. Red, black, yellow, golden, and apricot-colored, raspberries have been cultivated for the last 400 years. The red raspberry is the sturdiest and will stand the rigors of shipping. Other colors are usually not available at market and are best homegrown. The wild red raspberry is native to the northern states, while the black is native farther south.

Raspberries will be a brilliant color and shiny when ripe. They will literally fall off their stems and into the hand of the lucky picker. Different raspberries are in season throughout the summer. Reds generally precede blacks. Some varieties will yield fruit twice, in early summer and again in early fall. Red raspberries are high in vitamin A. Both black and red are a good source of vitamin C.

Strawberries. Strawberries will grow almost everywhere in the world, need little room, and multiply themselves by producing daughter plants. Strawberries can produce good crops without spraying because they bear fruit before pests get a good start.

Strawberries will color but not ripen off the vine. They should be picked when the fruit is a full bright red and shiny. To pick, pinch the stem between thumb and forefinger so that the berry is removed with stem intact. Never pull or pick strawberries from their stems. They will lose their vitamin content, become waterlogged and vulnerable to mold-causing bacteria. Strawberries are an excellent source of vitamin C.

Guidelines for Picking the Best Berries

Select berries that are plump and shiny, true to their variety's color. Stick with berries in season or purchase frozen. Straw-

berries in late November have traveled too far and been stored too long to be anything but a costly disappointment.

Avoid purchasing leaky or stained cartons that tell of damaged berries. Peek around and under the container to be sure that the choice berries have not just been strategically placed on top. Avoid moldy berries or those with a white cotton-like appearance. It's best if you can select the berries yourself from an open bin.

Storage at Home

Remove the berries from their container as soon as you can (even if you've picked them yourself). Sort through and remove any overripe or moldy berries so that they won't contaminate the others. Place the berries in a basket or dish lined with a paper towel. **Do Not Wash** until ready to use. Berries become "water logged" easily. Keep most berries in the refrigerator and plan to use within a day. Blueberries, cranberries, and currants have longer shelf lives (see chart on pages 8–11 for more specific information).

Berries that have become overripe or been kept too long are best made into sauce, syrup, or puree.

Handling

All berries, except the strawberry, should be free of their hull. The strawberry cap should be left on until ready to serve, to protect from collecting water and becoming soggy.

Just before serving, rinse berries quickly under cool water and spread out to dry on paper towels (away from sunlight).

Berry Information Chart

Berry	Characteristics	Cooking Qualities	Season
Blackberries (incl. dewberries, boysenberries, loganberries, olallieberries)	Purple, black, or blue-gray, seedy	Jam, tarts, cobblers, wine, baked goods, out of hand	Summer
Blueberries	Velvet blue, round with star opposite stem end	Jam, pie, muffins, baked goods, chutney, relishes, out of hand	Mid-late summer
Cranberries	Deep red, hard, tart berry	Relish, chutney, sauce, pies, tarts, baked goods	Late fall
Currants	Black, red, white, hard, tart berry	Jam, jelly, sauce, relish, dried	Mid-late summer
Elderberries	Black, hard, tart berry	Jam, jelly, wine	Early summer
Gooseberries	Most common is sharp green berry, also white, yellow, red berry	Green for jam, jelly, pies, tarts, others for eating out of hand	Late summer
Huckleberries	Deep blue, purple, resemble small blueberry	As blueberries jam, jellies, tarts, pies, baked goods, out of hand	Mid-late summer
Kiwifruit	Juicy brown, egg shape and size with brilliant green interior and tiny seeds	Jam, jelly, relish, tarts, poultry, fish, meat marinade out of hand	Spring-fall

Berry Information Chart

Selection Tips	Storage Handling	Vitamins/ Minerals	Calories per Serving
Shiny, plump berries without evidence of stem	Use immediately (within a day). Keep in a cool dry area or freeze up to 3 months.	Vitamins A & C	89 per cup
Firm, plump berries with good color	Store in refrigerator in tightly closed covered glass jar or freeze up to 6 months.	Vitamins A & C	90 per cup
Firm, plump berries with good color	Store in plastic bags in refrigerator up to 1 month or freeze up to 1 year.	Vitamin A & C	44 per cup
Firm, plump berries true to color	Store in plastic bags in refrigerator for up to 1 day.	Vitamin C	60 per cup
Firm, shiny berries	Use immediately.	Vitamin A	82 per cup
Hard, green berries	Use as soon as possible or freeze up to 3 months.	Vitamin C	59 per cup
Plump, richly colored berries	Use immediately or freeze up to 2 months.		90 per cup
Plump, slightly soft	Keeps in refrigerator up to 6 weeks. Most store-bought kiwifruit must be ripened at home a day or two at room temperature away from sunlight.	Vitamin C & Potassium	40 per fruit

(continued)

Berry Information Chart
(continued)

Berry	Characteristics	Cooking Qualities	Season
Raspberries	Black & red, should be shiny, pebbly-firm and of good color	Use in jam, jellies, tarts, pies, baked goods, out of hand	Summer-early fall
Strawberries	Full bright red berry, heart shaped, should be picked with stem in tact	Jelly, jam, tarts, pies, baked goods, out of hand	Spring-early summer

Oakley, Hugh, ed. *Buying Guide to Fresh Fruit and Vegetables.* 7th ed. Blue Goose, Inc., 1986.
The Packer 1987 Produce Availability and Merchandising Guide. XCII No. 53. Vance Publishing Corp., 1987. The Packer, P.O. Box 415, Prairie View, IL 60069,0415.

Freezing and Using

Freeze fresh berries if they will not be used within two days. Gently wash the berries under cool water, dry, and place on a cookie tray; when frozen, bag in freezer bag.

For sweeter frozen berries, sprinkle each with granulated sugar before placing on the cookie sheet. Fresh berry purees and sauces also freeze well (see individual berry recipes). Frozen freshly picked berries will keep up to six months. Berry purees and sauces and berries frozen with sugar will keep up to eight months.

In all of our recipes, you may use either fresh or *nonsweetened* frozen berries, unless otherwise specified. **Measure frozen berries, frozen.** Thawed berries become soft and pack down.

Berry Information Chart
(continued)

Selection Tips	Storage Handling	Vitamins/ Minerals	Calories per Serving
Plump, richly colored without stem end	Use immediately or freeze up to 2 months.	Vitamins A & C	Black, 98 per cup. Red, 70 per cup
Bright red berries, shiny and plump	Up to 3 days in the refrigerator or freeze.	Vitamin C	55 per cup

U.S. Department of Agriculture. Human Nutrition Information Service. Consumer Nutrition Center. *Composition of Foods: Fruits and Fruit Juices—Raw, Processed, Prepared.* Agriculture Handbook No. 8–9. S.E. Gebhardt et al., August 1982.

FROZEN BERRY QUANTITIES

2½ cups use 1 10-ounce bag, frozen
3 cups use 1 12-ounce bag, frozen
4 cups use 1 20-ounce bag, frozen

For Good Measure

It is difficult to give specific measurements for berries because the different sizes will determine how many fit into a pint or cup. A cup of large berries will contain less berries than a cup of smaller berries.

Blackberries
1 quart = 2 pints
1 pint = 2¼ cups
1 cup = ½ cup puree
Note: Loganberries and boysenberries are larger and there may be fewer berries per cup.

Blueberries
1 quart = 2 pints
1 pint = 2–2¼ cups
1 cup = ½ cup puree

Cranberries
1 quart = 2 pints
1 pint = 2–2¼ cups
1 cup = ½ cup puree

Currants (fresh)
1 quart = 2 pints
1 pint = 2 cups
1 cup = ½ cup puree

Elderberries
1 quart = 2 pints
1 pint = 2 cups
1 cup = ½ cup puree

Gooseberries
1 quart = 2 pints
1 pint = 2¼–2½ cups
1 cup = ½ cup puree

Huckleberries
1 quart = 2 pints
1 pint = 2 cups
1 cup = ½ cup puree

Kiwifruit
1 pound = 4–6 fruit
2 fruit = 1 cup sliced or diced
2 fruit = ½ cup puree

Mulberries
1 quart = 2 pints
1 pint = 2 cups
1 cup = ½ cup puree

Raspberries
1 quart = 2 pints
1 pint = 2 scant cups
1 cup = ½ cup puree

Strawberries
1 quart = 2 pints
1 pint = 20–30 strawberries or 2½ cups
1 cup = ½ cup puree

1 Berry Beverages

ot cranberry glug by the fire on a stormy night—tropical strawberry punch under the shade of a sun-drenched tree—what satisfying, refreshing berry concoctions. Whether it's a nutritious breakfast raspberry yogurt shake, a "coffee break" banana-blueberry smoothie, an evening high-tech cocktail, berries are the base that make the distinctive difference.

Frozen Berry Refresher

PREPARATION: 5 MINUTES.
SERVES 8.

1 6-ounce can frozen grapefruit juice, diluted
1 cup strawberries, partially thawed and mashed
1 cup raspberries, partially thawed and mashed
1 28-ounce club soda, chilled

Put all ingredients except club soda in the blender. Pour over crushed ice and top with club soda.

Bayfield, Wisconsin on Lake Superior celebrates strawberry season each year with Strawberry Days. Farmers' wives set out stands to sell freshly picked strawberries, strawberry pie, homemade ice cream, and fresh strawberry shortcake. The tiny port town comes to life with strolling musicians and evening fireworks.

Cranberry Shrub

PREPARATION: 5 MINUTES.
SERVES 8.

1 quart cranberry juice
2 cups sugar
rind of 1 lemon, in thin strips

½ cup white vinegar
1 quart soda water
1 pint fruit ice

In an enamel or glass pot, simmer cranberry juice, lemon rind, and sugar. Remove from heat. Add vinegar. Cool and refrigerate until cold. Fill tall glasses half-full of mixture, add soda water, and top with a scoop of fruit ice.

Cranberry Party Punch

PREPARATION: 10 MINUTES.
SERVES 12.

1 cup sugar
¾ cup water
1 quart cranberry juice
3 cups orange juice

¾ cup lemon juice
5 cups ginger ale
2 lemons, sliced
ice cubes for serving

Make sugar syrup by dissolving the sugar in water in a heavy-based pan. Stir until sugar is dissolved. Set aside to cool. Mix and chill juices. Just before serving, put juices and ice in punch bowl. Pour ginger ale over juices and ice. Sweeten to taste with sugar syrup. Float lemon slices in bowl.

The Indians introduced cranberries to the Pilgrims. In fact, they brought cranberries to the first Thanksgiving feast in 1621. The Indians cooked cranberries with honey and maple syrup, then dried them for winter storage. They also used cranberry juice to cure arrowhead wounds and to dye rugs and decorate blankets.

Spicy Cranberry Iced Tea

PREPARATION: 10 MINUTES.
SERVES 4–6.

6 teaspoons Ceylon tea
¼ teaspoon nutmeg
¼ teaspoon cinnamon
½ cup sugar

2 cups cranberry juice cocktail
½ cup orange juice
2 fresh lemons, squeezed
1½ cups ice water

Pour 3 cups of boiling water over the tea bags and spices. Steep 3–5 minutes. Add sugar. Cool. Add juices and ice water. Pour into ice-filled glasses.

Strawberry Lemonade

PREPARATION: 5 MINUTES.
MAKES 2 QUARTS.

4 cups strawberries
1 cup water
1 6-ounce can lemonade,
  undiluted

2 cups club soda

Put all ingredients except club soda in blender. Blend well. Fill glasses with cracked ice. Pour some syrup in each glass. Top with club soda and stir.

In the writing of Virgil, "the appearance of the first strawberries was a sure sign that summer had arrived."

Raspberry Yogurt Shake

PREPARATION: 5 MINUTES.
SERVES 2.

1 cup plain yogurt
½ cup milk
1 cup raspberries

3 ice cubes
sugar to taste

Put all ingredients in the blender and blend until the ice is well chopped.

Banana-Blueberry Smoothie

PREPARATION: 5 MINUTES.
SERVES 1.

1 cup blueberries
½ banana
⅔ cup skim milk

¼ teaspoon vanilla extract
2 ice cubes
sprinkle of cinnamon or nutmeg

Process all ingredients except ice cubes in blender or food processor. Add ice cubes. Sprinkle with nutmeg or cinnamon.

Buttermilk Kiwifruit Buster

PREPARATION: 5 MINUTES.
SERVES 4.

3 cups buttermilk
2 kiwifruit, pared and sliced

ice cubes

Pour buttermilk into blender or food processor. Peel kiwifruit and add to blender. Process until smooth. Pour over ice cubes.

Soothing Blackberry Mint Tea

PREPARATION: 10 MINUTES.
SERVES 4–6.

3 cups boiling water (use as it first boils to bring out excellent flavor in tea)
3 teaspoons loose tea

½ cup fresh mint leaves, crushed
2 cups blackberries
1 tablespoon honey or to taste

Pour boiling water over tea and mint leaves. Steep 5 minutes. Whirl blackberries in food processor or blender, sieve, and mash. Add mashed blackberries and honey to tea. Strain through a strainer before serving.

A blackberry is a dark black berry composed of many seeds. Grown commercially in the northern areas of the country, wild blackberries prefer the climate of the south and west. Blackberries are a favorite for jam. Boysenberries and loganberries, a member of the blackberry family, are similar in appearance but slightly tart in flavor.

Raspberry Champagne Punch

PREPARATION: 5 MINUTES.
MAKES 2½ QUARTS.

2 cups raspberries
⅓ cup fresh lemon juice
¼ cup sugar

1 quart rosé wine
1 quart raspberry sherbet
1 quart champagne

Puree raspberries in blender; combine with lemon juice, sugar, and wine. Stir to dissolve sugar. Just before serving, make small balls of sherbet with ice cream scoop. Add champagne.

Loganberries are named for Judge J.H. Logan, an amateur botanist, who grew the first berries in his garden in Santa Cruz. Loganberries make delicious wine.

STRAWBERRIES WITH SPIRITS

Strawberries and red or white wine, champagne, and a variety of liqueurs are spirited combinations. Kirsch, cherry, raspberry and blackberry brandy, kummel, Cointreau, and the best cognac are complementary partners. Champagne, port, and marsala are especially good with strawberries. Avoid overpowering flavors. Simply put fresh, hulled berries in individual glasses, sprinkle with sugar, then with the spirit.

It's the Berries!

The Elderberry tree is sometimes called the Judas tree and its blossom, the Judas blossom. According to one story, Christ's cross was made from elder wood and a Medieval tradition held that Judas hung himself from an elderberry tree.

Berry Burgundy

PREPARATION: 5 MINUTES.
MAKES 1 QUART.

2 cups berries of choice (blueberry, strawberry, raspberry, elderberry, gooseberry); reserve 1 cup

4 cups burgundy wine

Open burgundy wine 1 hour before serving. In four wine glasses, divide 1 cup of the berries for the bottom of the glasses. Press them with the back of a spoon. Pour wine over berries. Float reserved berries on top of wine. If they do not remain suspended, it does not matter for it is an unusual and attractive drink.

Berry Wine Cooler

PREPARATION: 2 MINUTES.
SERVES 1.

4 tablespoons strawberry puree
1 cup red wine, such as Beaujolais

club soda

For each cooler, fill glass with ice and puree, wine, and club soda. Garnish with lemon or lime slice.

Variation: Use champagne instead of club soda.

Huckleberry Brandy

PREPARATION: 15 MINUTES.
MAKES 5 QUARTS.

1½ gallons ripe huckleberries
2 pounds sugar

2 quarts brandy

Mash berries in food processor or blender to extract juice. Strain through double cheesecloth. Discard fruit. Boil juice and sugar, stirring to dissolve sugar. Add brandy. Store in sterile bottles with new corks.

Huckleberries grow in thick woods throughout Alaska, the Rockies, Montana, and along the Appalachian Trail. Sprawling thickets, huckleberry bushes produce glorious pink, urn-shaped flowers. Avid huckleberry pickers beware—these fragrant berries are favorites of bears.

Hot Buttered Cranberry Glug

PREPARATION: 25 MINUTES.
SERVES 5.

2 cups water
4 cups cranberries
1½ cups water
⅔ cup light brown sugar, packed
½ teaspoon ground cinnamon
½ teaspoon ground allspice

¼ teaspoon ground cloves
⅛ teaspoon ground nutmeg
1 18-ounce can unsweetened pine-apple juice
small dots of butter for serving cups

In a saucepan, cook cranberries in 2 cups of water until skins pop. Puree in a blender or food processor. Set aside. Bring 1½ cups water to a boil in the saucepan. Add brown sugar and spices; simmer 10 minutes to dissolve sugar. Add cranberry puree and pineapple juice; simmer 5 minutes. Keep hot until served. Put a small dot of butter on the top of each cup.

It's the Berries!

Blueberry Wine

PREPARATION: 10 MINUTES.
MAKES 1 GALLON.

1 gallon hot water
8 pints blueberries, put in an
   earthenware jar

3 pounds sugar

Pour hot water over berries. Let stand 3 days. Press out juice in double cheesecloth. Add 3 pounds of sugar. Allow it to sit 3 days stirring frequently to dissolve sugar. Strain and bottle in sterile jars and cork with clean corks. It will be ready in 6 months.

Mrs. Marsden's Grand Recipe for Gooseberry Wine (1843)

PREPARATION: 10 MINUTES.
MAKES 2 GALLONS.

1 gallon hot water
4 quarts gooseberries

3½ pounds sugar

Crush 4 quarts of berries to 1 gallon of water in a tub. Leave the berries in the tub 3 days. Poke and stir them with a long pole. Strain out liquid and save. Do not crush berries. Discard them. Add sugar. When the sugar is dissolved, barrel everything. Allow 6 months for liquid to clear. Add some liquid on hand if necessary.

Homemade Wines. In the 1800s, as the frontiers moved west, fruit wines were important because they preserved the harvest of the land. The berries that remained after all the jams and jellies had been put up were mashed, the juices were fermented, and they were used as medicine or for enjoyment. Gooseberries, raspberries, and currants were turned into popular sweet wines.

Black Currant Rum

PREPARATION: 10 MINUTES.
MAKES APPROXIMATELY 1 GALLON.

2 pounds black currants	5 cups white rum
6 blanched almonds	4 cups light brown sugar, packed

Wash fruit. Crush fruit and blanche almonds and place in a large wide sterile screwtop jar. Pour rum onto fruit and nuts. Seal and leave the jar in a cool place stirring daily. Using a fine sieve, strain off liquid into clean container. Put fruits and nuts into a linen bag and squeeze out as much remaining juice as possible. Discard fruit and nuts. Stir in sugar until dissolved. Bottle in sterile bottles. Leave for at least 6–12 months to mature.

Surprisingly, the black currant is a relative of the gooseberry rather than red or white currants. Banned in the United States because of a disease it carries that attacks white pine trees, it is in every European garden. Black currants have long been a home remedy for sore throats, feverish colds, and tonsillitis.

Crème De Cassis (Black Currant Liqueur)

PREPARATION: 10 MINUTES.
MAKES APPROXIMATELY 2 QUARTS.

1½ pounds ripe black currants	2–3 cloves
2 cups sugar	1 fifth-sized bottle brandy,
1 2-inch cinnamon stick	inexpensive

Crush black currants and sugar together, add spices and pour into sterile jar. Fill jar with brandy. Close tightly. Leave for a month in a sunny spot. After a month, strain through double cheesecloth. Put in a decanter. Keeps indefinitely.

Kir

PREPARATION: 2 MINUTES.
SERVES 1.

2 tablespoons Cassis (may purchase or see recipe on p. 22)

1 cup white wine, chilled

Serve in a wine glass.

Strawberry Punch

PREPARATION: 5 MINUTES.
SERVES 6–8.

4 cups strawberries
3 cups orange juice
1 quart ginger ale, chilled

1 12-ounce can frozen pineapple
  juice, diluted

Mix well and serve in a punch bowl.

Strawberries rinsed in white wine instead of water have a tangy flavor. A dash of vinegar heightens their sweetness, especially when sprinkled with confectioner's sugar.

TO MAKE A PUNCH ICE RING

To make a berry ice ring for punch, take a circle mold with a hole in the center. Fill to about one inch with a fruit juice of choice. Put a mixture of berries and mint leaves in the juice. Freeze. Add water to fill mold. Freeze until solid. To unmold, quickly dip in hot water. Turn into punch bowl.

---

2 Appetizers & Soups

*I*n the framework of the menu, the berry that appears usually at the end of the meal in dessert is equally delightful as a first course.

Some of the berry soups in this chapter were developed from the classic Scandinavian recipes of their origin. Others are inspirations of the New American cuisine.

We chose bright, colorful recipes for flashy entertaining and easy down-home dining. The "Christmas Holly Dip" makes a pretty addition to a holiday buffet. "Blueberry Soup" is a family favorite. Served up in glass mugs with a sprig of mint from the garden, it makes an elegant introduction to a simple shore supper of freshly grilled bluefish.

Kiwifruit Wrap-Ups

PREPARATION: 15 MINUTES.
SERVES 6.

½ pound prosciutto, thinly sliced   2½ pounds kiwifruit, peeled

Cut prosciutto in 1-inch strips. Cut kiwifruit in half lengthwise, quarter, and then cut in thin slices. Wrap pieces of prosciutto around kiwifruit slices. Secure with a toothpick.

The kiwifruit's roots reach back through history to China where this berry is known as the *Yang Tao*. The *Yang Tao* was eaten each day by the crew of trading junks for its "magic," (high vitamin content) which kept them from developing scurvy. There is more vitamin C in one kiwifruit than in a dozen oranges.

Kiwifruit, Cucumber, and Tuna Rounds

PREPARATION: 15 MINUTES.
MAKES 36 ROUNDS.

2 cucumbers, sliced in ¼-inch
  rounds
1 6½-ounce can tuna, drained

2 kiwifruit, peeled and diced
3 stalks celery, diced
3 tablespoons mayonnaise

Peel and cut cucumbers in ¼-inch rounds. Peel and dice kiwifruit, mince celery. Mix all ingredients together with mayonnaise. Mound onto cucumber rounds.

Strawberry-Cheddar Cocktail Ring

PREPARATION: 15 MINUTES.
SERVES 8–10.

1 pound sharp cheddar cheese
1 cup pecans, chopped
¾ cup mayonnaise
2 teaspoons strawberry vinegar
  (page 142)

1 onion, grated
1 clove of garlic, pressed
½ teaspoon Tabasco sauce
4 drops Worcestershire sauce
1 cup strawberry preserves

Blend all ingredients. Pour in small ring mold and chill. Fill center with strawberry preserves. Serve with water crackers.

American Indians were cultivating strawberries in 1643. The settlers going ashore in Massachusetts delighted in the species that abounded along the eastern seaboard and the northeastern continent. It was tiny, ruby red, and very sweet. California is now the leading producer of commercial strawberries.

Cranberry Bites

PREPARATION: 15–20 MINUTES.
MAKES 2½–3 CUPS SAUCE.
SERVES 6–8.

Cranberries are also called "bounce berries" because they bounce. Early American cooks sorted their berries by spilling them downstairs—those that bounced were keepers.

1 pound shrimp, cooked and peeled
1 pound chicken livers, cooked
1 20-ounce can pineapple chunks, drained; reserve ½ cup juice
1 cup cranberries

¾ cup cranberry juice
½ cup raspberry vinegar (page 140)
½ cup light brown sugar, packed
1 tablespoon cornstarch
2 tablespoons soy sauce

Mix pineapple juice, cranberry juice, raspberry juice, sugar, cornstarch, soy sauce, and cranberries. Cook over low flame until thick and glossy. Add shrimp, chicken livers, and pineapple. Toss gently and heat thoroughly. Serve in chafing dish.

Kiwifruit Shrimp Wheel

PREPARATION: 15 MINUTES.
SERVES 6.

1 pound shrimp, cooked, peeled, and chilled

8 kiwifruit, peeled and cut in long thin slices

Arrange shrimp and kiwifruit on a plate in the form of a pinwheel, alternating shrimp and kiwifruit. Marinate in dressing 4–6 hours in refrigerator. Drain. Serve on toothpicks.

Blueberry Vinaigrette Dressing:

PREPARATION: 15 MINUTES.
SERVES 6.

¾ tablespoon olive oil
¼ tablespoon blueberry vinegar (page 139)

½ teaspoon salt
¼ teaspoon prepared mustard

Combine all ingredients in a screwtop jar and shake until well blended.

Raspberry-Grapefruit Soup

PREPARATION: 10 MINUTES.
SERVES 6.

3 cups raspberries
3 cups grapefruit juice
1½ cups rosé wine

4 tablespoons honey or to taste
juice of 2 limes
1 cup sour cream

Puree ½ of raspberries in blender with grapefruit juice. Strain out seeds. Combine remaining raspberries, wine, honey, limes, and sour cream. Whisk briskly. Chill.

Berry of the Season Soup

PREPARATION: 15 MINUTES.
SERVES 6.

1 cup bland cookie or cake crumbs
  (vanilla wafers or pound cake)
4 cups of berries in season, rinsed
  (may be mixed or all of one
  kind)
juice of 1 lemon

4 cups cranraspberry juice
½ cup dry sherry
½ cup dry white wine
1 teaspoon ground ginger
1 teaspoon cinnamon
½ cup light cream

Pulverize cookie or cake crumbs to a very fine consistency. Place berries, lemon juice, sherry, and wine in saucepan and simmer until fruit is soft. Cool. When chilled, add juice, put in blender and add crumbs, ginger, and cinnamon. Mix well at low speed then high speed. Blend in cream. Served chilled.

Blueberries are very easy to grow, needing almost no care besides liking acid soil and good drainage. They will grow wherever azaleas, rhododendrons, and laurel grow.

Blueberry-Ginger Soup

PREPARATION: 15–20 MINUTES.
SERVES 6.

2 cups blueberries
3½ cups apple juice
1 10-ounce can frozen blueberry
juice, diluted with 1 10-ounce
can of water instead of 3

juice of 1 lemon
1 tablespoon freshly grated ginger
yogurt for garnish
cinnamon

Mix apple and cranberry juice in medium saucepan. Add blueberries and cook over medium heat until soft. Pour mixture into blender or food processor and puree until smooth. Chill at least 1 hour. Add fresh ginger. Serve with a dollop of yogurt and sprinkle with cinnamon on top of yogurt. Excellent with grilled poultry or fish.

Very Berry Soup

PREPARATION: 5 MINUTES.
SERVES 6.

3 cups strawberries
3 cups raspberries
1 21-ounce can cherry pie filling

4 cups cranraspberry juice
1 cup yogurt

Combine all ingredients and whisk briskly. This will make a light consistency and muddle the fruit. Chill. Excellent with a dollop of yogurt on each serving.

Blueberries are the third largest non-citrus fruit produced in the country. They grow almost everywhere on the continent and in Canada. Along the coast of Maine, blueberry pie is the classic finish to a clambake—steamers, lobsters, and corn on the cob. Blueberries and cranberries are members of the honeysuckle family.

Apricot-Raspberry Soup

PREPARATION: 10–15 MINUTES.
SERVES 6.

4 cups raspberries
4 cups apricot nectar
1 6-ounce jar strained apricot baby food
1 tablespoon cornstarch

2 tablespoons water
1 tablespoon orange zest
1 teaspoon cinnamon or nutmeg, if desired

Dissolve cornstarch in 2 tablespoons cold water. Heat apricot nectar with cornstarch until it thickens. Add raspberries, strained apricot baby food, orange zest, nutmeg, or cinnamon. Serve chilled.

Blueberry Soup

PREPARATION: 15 MINUTES.
SERVES 6.

2 cups blueberries
1½ cups sweet white wine
4 cups frozen blueberry juice, diluted; reserve ½ cup

juice from 1 lemon
2 tablespoons cornstarch
1 cup sour cream

Puree blueberries with wine and blueberry juice in a blender. Blend cornstarch into ½ cup blueberry juice. Heat over medium heat until slightly thickened and glossy—about 1 minute. Stir several times while cooling. Add lemon juice. Serve with a dollop of sour cream on each serving.

In Northern Europe, family expeditions into the woods in late summer are very popular. The growing locations of the wild blueberries are carefully guarded, and contests for those collecting the most berries are held. At sundown it is the one with the fullest berry basket who is held in high esteem, given a prize and an honorary title for the year.

Fruit Gazpacho

PREPARATION: 15 MINUTES.
SERVES 6.

2¼ cups tomato juice (1 quart)
¾ cup Bloody Mary mix
2 medium tomatoes, chopped
2 kiwifruit, peeled and chopped
¼ cup scallions
2 green peppers, chopped

2 tablespoons raspberry vinegar
  (page 140)
1 teaspoon lemon zest
2 tablespoons minced parsley, to
  top each serving
salt and pepper to taste

Chop tomatoes. Peel and chop kiwifruit, scallions, and peppers.
Add to tomato juice, Bloody Mary mix, vinegar, lemon zest,
salt, and pepper. Chill well. Before serving, mince parsley and
sprinkle over each serving.

Frieda Kaplan, owner of
Frieda's Finest, distributors of
exotic produce, introduced the
kiwifruit to supermarkets
more than 20 years ago.

Fruited Curry Consommé

PREPARATION: 10 MINUTES.
SERVES 6.

6 cups chicken broth
3 tablespoons cornstarch
½ cup scalded milk
2 tablespoons curry powder or to
  taste

4 cups blackberries
1 Granny Smith apple, cut in
  small cubes

Dissolve cornstarch in cold chicken broth. Add curry powder.
Heat until thick and clear. Add milk, blackberries, and apples.
Refrigerate overnight to allow flavors to develop. Heat to serv-
ing temperature.

Strawberry Tropical Soup

PREPARATION: 20–25 MINUTES.
SERVES 6.

3 cups strawberries
1 cup frozen cherries
4 cups frozen strawberry juice, diluted
2 tablespoons clover honey or to taste

⅓ cup fresh lime juice
½ cup sweet white wine
½ cup light cream
2 tablespoons cornstarch
2 tablespoons cold water
½ cup sour cream

Mix cornstarch in 2 tablespoons cold water. Simmer strawberry juice, honey, lime juice, and white wine until mixture thickens. Stir occasionally as it is cooling. Put strawberries and cream with chilled mixture and blend until smooth. Strain through a strainer. Mix in thawed cherries. Add a dollop of sour cream to each serving.

The strawberry was planted in Roman gardens and later cultivated by the French in the fourteenth century, and also by the Indians in North and South America. Our modern varieties of strawberry originated when a French military engineer named Frezier brought home plants of the large berries for breeding from Chile in the eighteenth century.

Strawberry Soup

PREPARATION: 10 MINUTES.
SERVES 6.

1½ cups strawberries
2 cups white grape juice
1 10-ounce can frozen strawberry juice, undiluted

1 cup skim milk
mint leaves for garnish

Put all ingredients in blender and puree. Chill. Garnish with mint, if available, before serving.

Christmas Holly Dip

PREPARATION: 15 MINUTES.
SERVES 8–10.

8 ounces cream cheese
½ cup corn syrup
½ cup sour cream
1 cup cranberries, chopped

4 tablespoons orange rind
1 tablespoon lemon rind
¼ cup chutney
holly for garnish

Beat cream cheese and syrup together until fluffy. Fold in remaining ingredients and place in serving dish. Make a hollow in center of dip and fill with chutney. Make 4–6 shallow trenches out from the hollow. Fill with chutney. Garnish with holly leaves. Serve with crackers or sliced apples.

3 Berry Entrées

From the time Liz sliced fresh strawberries instead of jelly onto my peanut butter sandwiches to an evening when we shared "Raspberry Shrimp Sauté" in the St. Paul Hotel, we've always believed berries deserve entrée attention.

If you're a turkey and cranberry devotee, wait until you try the "Flaming Raspberry Turkey Cutlets." You'll soon be anxious to try "Chicken Scallops with Kiwifruit and Peppers,"; the combinations are endlessly intriguing and delicious. Don't hesitate to experiment with your own favorite recipes and flavor combinations. We offer in this entire chapter our latest discoveries, along with some lifetime favorites.

Cranberry Pork Chops

PREPARATION: 15 MINUTES.
BAKE 1 HOUR.
SERVES 6.

6 pork chops
4 cups cranberries, chopped
1 medium onion, chopped

1 cup honey
salt and pepper to taste

Preheat oven to 350°F. In a large skillet brown chops on both sides over medium heat. Salt and pepper to taste. Combine cranberries, onion, and honey. Put chops in an oven-proof casserole. Spread cranberry mixture on top of chops. Cover.

Cranberry comes from the Dutch word *kranberre*. Others claim that it gets its name from crane berry because the plant's flower is shaped like a crane. Cranes and cranberries are both at home in bogs. Indians called it bitter berry.

Kiwifruit Chicken

PREPARATION: 35 MINUTES.
SERVES 3–4.

2 tablespoons olive oil
2 cups red onions, thinly sliced
salt and pepper to taste
2 medium boned, skinned chicken
   breasts
2 tablespoons corn oil

2 kiwifruit, peeled
¼ pound ham
¼ cup white wine
¼ cup cranberry juice
1 teaspoon thyme
1 teaspoon rosemary

Heat skillet and add olive oil. Cook onions until golden brown. Transfer to a plate. Cut chicken breasts in ½-inch wide strips. Cook chicken strips until cooked through. Remove to plate with onions. Cut ham in thick slices, then long strips. Add ham to warm skillet, and sauté slightly. Cut kiwifruit in circles, then quarters. Add kiwifruit and warm gently. Remove to plate. Deglaze pan with wine, cranberry juice, thyme, and rosemary. Reduce sauce. Return chicken, ham, onions, and kiwifruit. Warm through gently to serving temperature.

Cranberry juice was not marketed nationwide until 1967. Homemade cranberry juice is simple to make and keeps several months if refrigerated. New Englanders have been enjoying it for 350 years.

Chicken Scallops with Kiwifruit and Peppers

PREPARATION: 45 MINUTES.
SERVES 8.

4 chicken breasts, boned, split in half	2 red peppers, cut in thin strips
flour	½ cup sweet white wine
salt	¼ cup heavy cream
pepper	2 tablespoons clarified butter
	2 kiwifruit peeled, cut in chunks

Pound chicken breasts between waxed paper until thin. Dredge in flour, salt, and pepper. Seed peppers and cut in ¼-inch strips. Heat butter in skillet until melted. Add chicken when butter bubbles. Sauté chicken, cover, and cook about 30 minutes. Remove chicken and pan juices to warm platter. Skim fat. Add and sauté pepper strips. Deglaze pan with wine. Cook down to syrup consistency. Lower heat. Add cream. Return scallops and pepper strips to pan. Gently heat through. Garnish scallops with kiwifruit chunks.

Kiwifruit can be easily peeled if you dip them in boiling water for a few seconds.

Cranberry-Mustard Chicken Breasts

PREPARATION: 50 MINUTES.
SERVES 8.

4 whole chicken breasts, boned
  and skinned
flour
salt
pepper
1 large onion, chopped
¼ cup clarified butter

½ cup orange juice
½ cup heavy cream
¼ cup cranberries, chopped
¼ cup cognac
4 tablespoons coarse mustard
1 tablespoon cornstarch

Melt butter in a large skillet. Cut chicken breasts in half. Pound breasts between waxed paper to even thickness of meat. Dredge in flour, salt, and pepper. Cook breasts over medium heat—12 minutes each side. Transfer to warm plate. Sauté onion until translucent. Skim fat from pan. Combine orange juice, cream, chopped cranberries, cognac, mustard, and cornstarch. Cook over medium heat until thickened. Return breasts to pan. Turn to coat in sauce before serving.

The cranberry is a major crop of Massachusetts, New Jersey, Wisconsin, and Oregon. Cranberry bogs are sandy and marshy. They can remain productive after a century. In New England, bogs are picked between Labor Day and the end of October. The harvest of cranberries is a splendid sight. Water is let into bogs and the cranberries (that have been mechanically detached) float to collecting points on the water's edge.

Chicken with Strawberry Vinegar and Honey

PREPARATION: 50 MINUTES.
SERVES 8.

4 pounds of chicken, quartered
salt and pepper to taste
2 tablespoons clarified butter
2 tablespoons peanut oil, plus
 some to sauté shallots
4 shallots, minced

½ cup strawberry vinegar (page
 142)
⅓ cup honey
1 cup strawberries, hulled and
 rinsed or if frozen drained
 and thawed, sliced

Rinse and dry chicken. Sprinkle with salt and pepper to taste. Combine butter and oil in large skillet, add chicken and brown. (Do not crowd pieces.) When chicken has been browned, remove to a warm platter with pan juices. Skim fat. Sauté shallots in a small amount of oil until translucent. Add strawberry vinegar and honey to pan and simmer. Return chicken, cook partially covered for about 20 minutes. Baste often to glaze chicken. Toss in strawberries just before serving.

William Butler once said of the strawberry, "Doubtless God could have made a better berry, but doubtless God never did."

Curried Chicken

PREPARATION: 30 MINUTES.
SERVES 8.

2 pounds chicken breast, boned,
   skinned, and cut in 1-inch cubes
flour
salt
pepper
3 tablespoons butter
½ cup onion, chopped
½ cup celery, diagonally sliced
3 medium tomatoes, chopped *or*
   1 8-ounce can crushed tomatoes in tomato sauce

2 tablespoons butter
2 tablespoons flour
1 cup light cream
3 teaspoons curry powder or to
   taste
1 banana cut in circles, then
   quarters
2 cups blueberries
2 cups shredded coconut

Dredge chicken in flour, salt, and pepper. Heat butter in frying pan. Sauté chicken chunks, a few at a time. Do not brown. Remove to warm plate. Sauté onion and celery until translucent. Remove to warm plate. Melt butter in pan. Add flour. Gradually add cream, stirring constantly. Add curry powder. When this sauce is thickened, return chicken, celery, onions, and tomatoes to pan. Heat to serving temperature. Toss in bananas and blueberries. Sprinkle shredded coconut on top.

Blueberries are believed to have been grown and harvested by prehistoric tribes. Excavations of Neolithic and Iron Age sites have unearthed stores of harvested seeds.

It's the Berries!

Chicken Livers with Blueberry-Lemon Vinegar

PREPARATION: 25 MINUTES.
SERVES 8.

2 pounds chicken livers
flour
salt
pepper
2 tablespoons clarified butter
1 medium onion, chopped

1 tablespoon freshly grated ginger
⅓ cup blueberry-lemon vinegar
  (page 139)
½ cup sour cream
1 cup blueberries, rinsed

Dredge chicken livers in flour, salt, and pepper. Melt butter in frying pan. Sauté livers until almost firm to the touch. Remove to a warm plate. Add onion to frying pan. Sauté until translucent. Remove to warm plate. Deglaze pan with blueberry vinegar. Lower heat and stir in sour cream. **Do Not Boil.** Return liver and onions to pan. Toss and coat over low heat until warmed through. Add blueberries and toss gently.

Flaming Raspberry Turkey Cutlets

PREPARATION: 20–25 MINUTES.
SERVES 8.

8 turkey cutlets
4 tablespoons butter
2 teaspoons raspberry vinegar
    (page 140)
½ cup raspberry juice, undiluted

1 teaspoon sugar
4 tablespoons raspberry brandy,
    Crème de Framboise
1 cup raspberries

Pound turkey between waxed paper to an even thickness. Sauté turkey breasts in butter in a large skillet. Turn once. Cutlets are cooked if juices run clear when pronged with a fork. Remove and cover to keep warm. Deglaze skillet with vinegar. Add raspberry concentrate and sugar. Return cutlets to skillet. Warm raspberry brandy. Add warm brandy and light with match to flame. This can be done just before serving for a spectacular presentation. Add the raspberries to sauce before serving.

The berry seed is surrounded by a sweet protecting pulp and skin. Each berry is a power-packed capsule rich in vitamins, minerals, fiber, and natural sugars. Berries have large amounts of vitamins A, B, and C.

Cranberry and Turkey Crumb Pie

PREPARATION: 15–20 MINUTES.
BAKE 30 MINUTES.
SERVES 4–6.

2 tablespoons butter
3 tablespoons flour
¾ cup chicken broth
1½ cups cooked turkey meat, cut in chunks
2½ cups mushrooms, sliced

1 cup celery, diagonally sliced
½ cup cranberries, chopped
3 tablespoons sherry
½ cup cream
juice of 1 lemon
2 cups bread cubes or crumbs

Preheat oven to 350°F. Butter a medium casserole. Melt butter over low flame. Add flour, make a paste. Gradually add chicken broth and milk. Cook until thickened. Add turkey and other ingredients. Cook over low heat for a few minutes. Spread bread cubes over mixture. Bake in preheated oven.

An old Cape Cod legend explains how the country's best cranberry bogs came to be: An Indian medicine man cast a spell over the Reverend Richard Bourne and then mired him in quicksand. For the following two weeks the two waged a battle of wits. The minister was sustained only by a white dove who fed him cranberries. The Indian fell exhausted and the spell was lifted. One of the berries fell to the ground and became rooted forever in the Cape Cod soil. Half the annual crop of cranberries in the United States comes from Massachusetts were cultivation began in 1840.

Blackberry Cornish Game Hens

PREPARATION: 10 MINUTES.
BAKE 1 HOUR.
SERVES 6.

6 Cornish game hens
salt
pepper
lemon juice
4 tablespoons melted butter

1 cup blackberry jam
¼ cup sherry
2 tablespoons Dijon-style mustard
1 cup blackberries; reserve

Preheat oven to 425°F. Rub hens inside and out with salt, pepper, and lemon juice. Coat hens with butter and place in preheated oven. Reduce heat after 20 minutes to 350°F.

Prepare glaze: Combine all remaining ingredients and simmer until jam has melted and sauce is glossy. After 25 minutes, remove birds from oven. Coat each bird with glaze. Return to finish cooking. Brush frequently for the remaining 15 minutes. Just before serving, gently stir berries into glaze. Spoon over birds. Pass remaining glaze separately.

Rock Cornish game hens are the result of patient crossbreeding of Cornish gamecocks and Plymouth Rock hens. These plump little birds are all white meat and a mild, gamy flavor, due in part to their diet that includes acorns and cranberries.

Raspberry-Currant Glazed Duck

PREPARATION: 10 MINUTES.
BAKE 1¾–2 HOURS (20 MINUTES PER POUND).
SERVES 3–4.

1 5–6 pound duck	½ cup honey
½ cup currant jelly	2 tablespoons Cassis
½ cup raspberry jam	1 cup raspberries

Preheat oven to 450°F. Rub duck with garlic. Place on rack in roasting pan. Place in oven. Reduce heat to 350°F.

In a small saucepan, combine jelly, jam, honey, and Cassis over low heat. Just before duck is finished cooking, remove from oven. Coat duck with glaze and return to oven 10–15 minutes until glaze carmelizes. Remove from oven and allow to stand 10 minutes. Garnish with raspberries just before serving.

Most of the currants in the United States are imported as they carry a parasite that attacks the white pine tree. If currants are available fresh, the season is June to August.

Teriyaki Steak Strips

PREPARATION: 15 MINUTES.
SERVES 8.

2 pounds flank steak

Partially freeze beef and cut in thin slices across grain. After slicing, marinate meat strips for 6 hours. Weave meat on skewer and grill over grill or under broiler. Cook to medium-rare. Garnish with raspberries. Also, can weave meat, pepper chunks, mushroom caps, and cherry tomatoes on to skewers and make kebabs.

Raspberry-Ginger Marinade:

¼ cup raspberry-ginger vinegar
  (page 141)
½ cup soy sauce
½ cup peanut oil
¼ cup orange juice

1 tablespoon honey
1 shallot, minced
1 tablespoon fresh ginger, minced
1 cup raspberries

In medium-sized bowl, combine ingredients for marinade.

The Indians taught the settlers not only the joy of eating berries found in their new land but also the secrets of using them for herbal medicines and dyes.

Cranberry Pot Roast

PREPARATION: 15–20 MINUTES.
BAKE 3 HOURS.
SERVES 8–10.

4 pounds beef chuck or
   rump roast
flour
salt
pepper
1 16-ounce can cranberry sauce

1 cup apple juice
4 tablespoons oil
2-inch strip orange peel, orange
   part only
2 tablespoons flour

Preheat oven to 325°F. Dredge meat in flour, salt, and pepper. In a skillet brown meat in oil. When brown on all sides, pour off fat. Add cranberry sauce, apple juice, and orange rind. Cover. Bake in preheated oven. When baking, add water occasionally if necessary. When fork tender, remove meat to a warm platter. Skim fat from pan juices. Cool 2 cups of pan juices and add flour. Return to pan and cook over low heat until thickened for gravy. Return meat to pan and heat to serving temperature.

Commercial cultivation of the cranberry began by accident in about 1816. Henry Hall, of Cape Cod noticed that the bogs that had sand blown over them produced a better berry. Cranberries were among the first fruit to be commercially canned by Underwood and sold for $1.50 per can.

Veal Scallopini with Kiwifruit

PREPARATION: 30 MINUTES.
SERVES 6.

1½ pounds veal cutlet
flour
salt
pepper
2 tablespoons peanut oil
2 tablespoons butter
2 shallots, minced

1½ cups apple juice
2 tablespoons cornstarch blended
    with ¼ cup water
¼ cup chicken broth
3 ripe kiwifruit, peeled and sliced
    in thin rounds

Pound veal between waxed paper to ¼ inch thick. Dredge in flour, salt, and pepper. Melt butter and peanut oil in pan and brown cutlets, a few at a time. Remove and keep warm. Add shallot and cook until limp. Add half of apple juice and scrape pan. Return veal to pan and cover over medium heat 5 minutes or until tender. Remove veal to heated platter. Add cornstarch-water mixture, chicken broth, and reserved apple juice. (Add more apple juice if necessary to have adequate sauce for cutlets.) Return cutlets to pan. Turn to coat with sauce. Serve cutlets with kiwifruit divided, and placed on top of each. Spoon remaining sauce over top of kiwifruit and cutlets.

Kiwifruit is a rich source of vitamin C and, like pineapple has the curious property of tenderizing meat.

Berry Burgers

PREPARATION: 15 MINUTES.
BAKE 20–30 MINUTES.
SERVES 6.

1½ pounds ground lean beef
1 egg, beaten
1 medium onion, chopped
½ cup bread crumbs
½ cup milk

1 tablespoon Worcestershire sauce
1 16-ounce can cranberry sauce
¼ cup brown sugar, packed
3 tablespoons raspberry vinegar
  (page 140)

Preheat oven to 350°F. Mix meat, egg, onion, bread crumbs, milk, and Worcestershire sauce and form into individual patties. Do not overmix. Put patties in an oven-proof dish. Combine cranberry sauce, sugar, and vinegar in blender or food processor and mix well. Cover meat patties with mixture. Bake in preheated oven. Baste occasionally. Serve with sauce spooned over burgers.

The cranberry was originally known as the fenberry in England—a fen is a swampy place, and cranberries grow best in "swamp places."

Glazed Ham with Blackberry Sauce

PREPARATION: 15 MINUTES.
BAKE HAM 2¼–2½ HOURS.
SERVES 10–14.

1 5–7 pound boneless, smoked whole ham
1 12-ounce can beer
½ cup brown sugar, packed
⅓ cup Dijon-style mustard
1 8-ounce can crushed pineapple, drained; reserve juice
1 6-ounce can frozen orange juice, undiluted
1 tablespoon cornstarch, dissolved in ¼ cup water
2 cups blackberries

Preheat oven to 325°F. Place ham in roasting pan and bake in preheated oven.

In a small saucepan, combine beer, sugar, mustard, reserved pineapple juice, and orange juice. Add cornstarch mixture. Cook over low heat until glossy. When ham is ready to be served, skim off any fat. Turn oven to 450°F. Coat ham with glaze. Add berries and pineapple to sauce and pour over ham just before serving.

One of the oldest recorded berries—blackberries have flourished for centuries. Blackberry seeds have been found in the remains of Neolithic man dug up in Essex, England.

Currant-Mustard Glazed Ham

PREPARATION: 10 MINUTES.
BAKE 12–15 MINUTES PER POUND.
AVERAGES 20 SERVINGS (¼ POUND PER PERSON).

5 pound canned ham
1 8-ounce jar currant jelly
¼ cup steak sauce
1 tablespoon brown sugar

1 tablespoon corn oil
2 tablespoons prepared mustard
1 cup dried currants, soaked in
   warm water to "plump" up

Preheat oven to 325°F. Put ham in roasting pan. In a small saucepan, combine ingredients for glaze. Simmer to melt jelly. Pour glaze over ham 30 minutes before serving time. Serve extra glaze on the side.

Cranberries are high in vitamin C. The berries were taken in crates by the whalers and doled out in handfuls on long voyages to prevent scurvy.

Fish Fillets with Orange Raspberry Sauce

PREPARATION: 20 MINUTES.
SERVES 6–8.

6 flounder fillets or any white fish
1 cup buttermilk
flour
salt

pepper
1 tablespoon clarified butter
1 tablespoon peanut oil

Dip fillets in buttermilk, dredge in flour, salt, and pepper. Set aside and assemble. Melt butter and oil in large skillet. Sauté fillets until golden brown. When fillets are done, transfer to warm plates and spoon sauce over each.

Raspberry-Orange Sauce:

1½ cups orange juice
2 tablespoons cornstarch
2 teaspoons orange zest
2 tablespoons mayonnaise

1 cup raspberries rinsed, or if frozen, thawed, drained, and mashed

Combine orange juice, cornstarch, and zest in saucepan. Cook over low heat until thick and glossy. Add mayonnaise and raspberries.

Keep warm in double boiler.

Thimbleberries look something like small raspberries, and are found along the Great Lakes, in the Rockies, the coast of California and Oregon, and in Alaska.

It's the Berries!

Stir-Fried Shrimp with Raspberry Vinegar

PREPARATION: 35 MINUTES.
SERVES 6–8.

oil to coat wok
2 peppers (1 red, 1 green) seeded
  and cut in diagonal strips
1 medium onion, cut in strips
2 pounds shrimp, shelled and
  deveined

1 can water chestnuts, sliced
2 cups pea pods
1 16-ounce can pineapple chunks,
  drained; reserve juice
1 cup raspberries

Coat wok with oil. Heat until drop of water spatters. Stir-fry peppers and onions until just "crunchy." Remove to side. Add shrimp in small batches. Stir-fry until shrimp change color to pink. Remove to side. Add sauce to wok and cook over low heat until glossy. Add water chestnuts, pea pods, and pineapple chunks. Toss in sauce. Add vegetables and shrimp, stirring and tossing until serving temperature. **Do Not Overcook.** Toss in raspberries just before serving for garnish. Can be served with Chinese cellophane noodles, fresh raspberry sherbet, and almond cookies.

Sauce:

2 tablespoons brown sugar
1 tablespoon cornstarch
½ teaspoon chili powder
½ teaspoon ground ginger
1½ cups water

reserved pineapple juice
3 tablespoons catsup
1 tablespoon soy sauce
1 tablespoon raspberry vinegar
  (page 140)

In small bowl, combine all sauce ingredients. Set aside.

To pick, pinch the stem between thumb and forefinger so that the berry is removed with stem intact—never pull or pick berries from their stem.

Piquant Fish Steaks

PREPARATION: 10 MINUTES.
BAKE 20 MINUTES.
MAKES 1¼ CUPS SAUCE.

Swordfish steaks, 1 inch thick (allow ¼ pound per person)

¼ cup melted butter
4 tablespoons lemon juice

Preheat oven to 350°F. Grease large baking dish. Arrange steaks in pan. Combine lemon juice with butter and drizzle over fish.

Piquant Sauce:

¼ cup butter, melted
2 tablespoons strawberry vinegar (page 142)

1 tablespoon grated lemon zest
1 cup strawberries, mashed with fork

While fish is cooking, assemble sauce. Heat sauce gently to serving temperature and spoon over fish just before serving. Fresh tuna or cod steaks can be substituted and are equally delicious.

Today, our commercial strawberry is a hybrid of the large Chilean strawberry and the small Virginia strawberry, developed in 1821 by botanist Nicholas Duchane.

Gingery Fish with Kiwifruit

PREPARATION: 15 MINUTES.
SERVES 8.

2 pounds fish fillets (¼ pound
  each)
oil to coat broiling pan
2 tablespoons freshly grated ginger
1 clove of garlic, minced

½ cup teriyaki sauce
⅛ stick butter, cut in pieces
2 kiwifruit peeled, cut in rounds
  then quarters

Preheat broiler. Lightly oil broiler pan. Pierce surface of fish with a sharp fork. Spread ginger over fillets and rest fish a few minutes to allow ginger to penetrate. Combine garlic and teriyaki. Dot fish with butter and run under broiler for 5 minutes. Pour the garlic-teriyaki mixture over fish and continue to broil until fish is translucent and flaky. Scatter kiwifruit over fish and run under broiler to heat through.

Jersey Shore Eggs

PREPARATION: 15 MINUTES.
SERVES 6.

6 hard-boiled eggs, peeled and
    sliced in rounds; set aside
1 10-ounce package frozen
    crabmeat, thawed and drained

6 slices French bread, sliced
    ½ inch thick and toasted
1 pound mozzarella cheese, grated

To assemble eggs, place egg slices on toasted French bread on a baking sheet. Spoon crabmeat onto eggs. Pour sauce over crabmeat and eggs. Scatter blueberries over sauce. Top with mozzarella and run under broiler to melt cheese.

Sauce:

2 tablespoons butter, melted
2 tablespoons flour
1 cup milk
3 tablespoons Dijon-style mustard

2 tablespoons blueberry vinegar
    (page 139)
1 cup blueberries

Melt butter in saucepan over low heat. Blend in flour, then mustard. Cook over low heat stirring constantly until smooth. Add vinegar and milk. Keep warm in double boiler.

4 Significant Salads

S imply put, Beth and I are salad fanatics, constantly tossing up wild combinations. And why not? Of all culinary categories, salads are well suited to carefree creativity—fresh vegetables, fresh seafood from the market, last night's grilled chicken—whatever is in season and in the cupboard.

Here are our favorite salad entrées for light and hearty meals, spectacular side dishes, and simple tossed greens with berry vinegars. We've included traditional make-ahead gelatin molds and fruit salads plus vinaigrettes, salad splashes, and dressings.

An Aside on Salad Dressings

In the dressing recipes that accompany these salad recipes, we call for berry vinegars as ingredients. Berry vinegars are a cinch to make (see Chapter 9) and will keep several months.

You may choose to substitute with store-bought berry vinegars *or* with mild wine vinegars like rice wine vinegar, champagne vinegar, or good quality white wine vinegar.

If in doubt, substitute lemon juice for the vinegar we've specified. A poor quality or strong vinegar (malt vinegar, distilled white vinegar, or cider vinegar, for example) will overpower the balanced flavors in the dressing and the salad.

Blackberries, according to the Oxford Dictionary, "'Tis being the commonest wild fruit in England is spoken of proverbally as the type of that which is plentiful and little prized."

Blueberry, Beet, and Horseradish Mold

PREPARATION: 20 MINUTES.
SERVES 6–8.

1 tablespoon plain gelatin	¾ cup celery, chopped
½ cup cold water	2 tablespoons onion, minced
1 16-ounce can diced beets	2 tablespoons horseradish
drained; reserve 1 cup liquid	1 tablespoon sugar
½ cup fresh lemon juice	salad greens for base

Sprinkle gelatin over ½ cup cold water in bowl. Heat the reserved beet juice and lemon juice. Pour over gelatin and stir to dissolve. Add celery, onion, sugar, and horseradish. Add blueberries. When the gelatin mixture is thickened, pour into a 1-quart oiled mold. Refrigerate until firm. Unmold onto salad greens of choice.

The peak period to buy blueberries: June, July, and August. Look for large, dry, plump, powdery berries. Check the bottom of the container; straining indicates crushed or old fruit. Eat immediately to savor the full flavor.

Currant and Carrot Salad

PREPARATION: 5 MINUTES.
SERVES 2–3.

2 cups currants	salt
4 large carrots, coarsely chopped	pepper
2–3 teaspoons sugar	lettuce or romaine for garnish
juice of 1 lemon	

Toss currants and carrots, sugar, and lemon. Taste for salt or pepper. Arrange on bed of romaine or lettuce.

Strawberry Chicken Salad with Poppyseed Dressing

PREPARATION: 15 MINUTES.
MAKES 1¼ CUPS.
SERVES 6–8.

2½ cups white meat chicken, cut
  in chunks
2 cups strawberries
2 cups honeydew melon, scooped
  into balls

3 cups spinach, torn
3 cups romaine lettuce, torn
1 head endive, shredded (dry
  greens thoroughly)

Combine and gently toss to mix all salad ingredients except endive. Drizzle dressing over and toss gently again. Scatter splintered endive over top.

Poppyseed Dressing:

¾ cup oil
¼ cup blueberry vinegar (page
  139)
1 tablespoon sugar
2 teaspoons onion, minced

1 teaspoon salt
1 teaspoon dry mustard
1 tablespoon poppyseeds
2 tablespoons orange juice
zest strips of 1 lemon

Combine all ingredients in blender or tightly lidded jar and blend.

In the United States few people bothered to cultivate berries. Wild berries were plentiful and the strawberry patch was everywhere. Early in the nineteenth century a demand for strawberries served with cream surfaced. President Martin Van Buren loved them, eating them with each meal. He was criticized for growing them for his table with public funds.

Kiwifruit Tuna Salad

PREPARATION: 15 MINUTES.
SERVES 6–8.

3 6½-ounce cans tuna, drained
2 tablespoons snipped chives

3 kiwifruit, peeled and chopped
8 tablespoons slivered almonds

Toss all ingredients with Raspberry Mayonnaise (see below)

Raspberry Mayonnaise:

1 egg yolk
1 teaspoon prepared mustard
2 tablespoons raspberry vinegar
(page 140)

1 cup olive oil
3 tablespoons frozen raspberry
juice concentrate, undiluted
⅓ cup sour cream

In a blender or food processor, combine egg yolk, mustard, and vinegar. Add oil, with motor running, in a slow steady stream and process until thick. Add remaining ingredients. Salt and pepper to taste.

The Salmonberry, a salmon-colored raspberry, can be found in the Aleutian Islands, Kodiak Isle and on the northern coast of California.

Kiwifruit and Pasta Salad

PREPARATION: 20 MINUTES.
SERVES 6–8.

1½ cups cooked chicken
3 cups ziti
1 tablespoons salad oil
2 kiwifruit, peeled, cut in rounds
   then quartered

8 cherry tomatoes, cut in half
1 green pepper, cut in chunks
1 cup frozen peas, thawed

Cut chicken in chunks and set aside. Cook ziti to *al dente* stage in large pot of boiling salted water. Add salad oil to the water. Drain, rinse under cold water and chill. Gently toss chicken, kiwifruit, tomatoes, peppers, and thawed peas with Raspberry Sour Cream Dressing.

Raspberry Sour Cream Dressing:

1 egg yolk
1 teaspoon prepared mustard
2 tablespoons raspberry vinegar
   (page 140)

1 cup oil
½ cup sour cream

In a blender put egg yolk, mustard, and vinegar. Add oil in a very thin stream until mayonnaise thickens. Add sour cream. Chill.

The kiwifruit's unattractive exterior is a hoax! Its fuzzy, khaki exterior hides a large berry, tart in flavor, vibrant chartreuse in color, with a starburst circle of tiny jet black seeds.

Bean and Blueberry Salad

PREPARATION: 20 MINUTES.
SERVES 10–12.

1 16-ounce can of black beans
1 16-ounce can of red kidney
  beans
1 16-ounce can of chick peas
2 tablespoons olive oil
2 tablespoons corn oil
1 large Spanish onion, chopped
1 red pepper, seeded and chopped
1 green pepper, seeded and
  chopped

1 clove of garlic, crushed
1 cup blueberry-lemon vinegar
  (page 139)
1½ tablespoons clover honey or 2
  tablespoons sugar
1 teaspoon salt
1 cup blueberries

Heat beans in their liquid. Heat oils in frying pan and cook onion, peppers, and garlic until translucent. Drain beans from their liquid. Drain oil from frying pan. Add beans to onion and pepper. Remove garlic. Pour vinegar and honey or sugar over all ingredients and add salt. Stir. Cover and simmer 5–15 minutes. Toss in blueberries just before serving. Keeps well for several days.

On summer Sundays, I remember being a camper, dressed in green and white uniforms, walking two by two, on a dusty road to the small white clapboard chapel near the shore in Maine.

After the service, the hymns ringing in our ears, and hunger pangs hurrying us toward "Sunday Chicken and Rice" at camp, we eagerly looked for dust covered, tiny wild blueberries that fringed the road—velvet blue with the same dust that covered our moccasins. We'd gently pick them from their sage green bower, rolling them around our tongue, before snapping their sweet-tart flavor with our teeth.

It's the Berries!

Beet and Blueberry Salad

PREPARATION: 15 MINUTES (PLUS 2 HOURS TO MARINATE BEETS).
SERVES 6–8.

Whortleberries, blaeberries, or whinberries are closely related to the blueberry. The main difference is that the whortleberry is a little plant no more than 18 inches tall and usually produces berries singly and not in clusters as cultivated berries do.

1 16-ounce can of shoestring beets
5 Belgian endive
5 bunches watercress, rinsed, dried, and stems discarded

3 carrots, shredded
2 cups blueberries

Drain and rinse beets in cold water. Marinate in blueberry-orange vinaigrette dressing for 2 hours for a fuller flavor. Separate and trim leaves of endive. Reserve the best leaves to be used whole. Slice and sliver the remaining leaves. Serve on 6–8 salad plates; lay endive leaves in a circle. Place watercress next in a circle to form a nest for the beets and carrots. Drain beets from marinade. Toss beets and carrots together. Place beets and carrots in salad greens nest. Make well, or indentation in this mixture and fill with blueberries. Sprinkle endive slivers over each plate. Drizzle dressing over salad. Serve well chilled.

Blueberry-Orange Vinaigrette Dressing:

½ cup salad oil
¼ cup blueberry-orange vinegar (page 142)

1½ teaspoon Dijon-style mustard
1 teaspoon yogurt

In a small bowl, whisk together salad dressing ingredients, reserve until salad is assembled.

Strawberry Onion Salad

PREPARATION: 15 MINUTES.
SERVES 6.

leaves of spinach and romaine
    for base of salad
8 slices red onion, thinly sliced
    and separated

20 strawberries

On separate serving plates make a bed of spinach and romaine leaves. Place the onion rings on spinach and romaine. Mound the strawberries on onions. Drizzle with dressing.

Dressing:

1 cup mayonnaise
¼ cup frozen strawberry juice con-
    centrate, undiluted

½ teaspoon poppyseed

Whisk together ingredients for dressing.

Imagine strawberries, raspberries, blueberries, grapes, or banana slices frozen on a tray. Remove a few minutes before eating—pop in your mouth, like candy.

Raspberry Avocado Salad

PREPARATION: 15 MINUTES.
SERVES 4.

1 avocado, ripe
radicchio
watercress

1 pint fresh raspberries
2 tablespoons lemon juice

Peel and quarter avocado and dip in lemon juice to keep from browning. Wash and dry radicchio and lettuce. Make a bed of radicchio and lettuce on each plate. Arrange avocado in center and top with raspberries. Just before serving, drizzle Raspberry Vinaigrette overall. A wonderful accompaniment to duck dishes.

Raspberry Vinaigrette:

⅔ cup olive oil
⅓ cup raspberry vinegar (page 140)

1 teaspoon salt
1 teaspoon sugar

Whisk together and reserve until serving.

Yellow and amber raspberries have even more intense and more mellow flavor then red raspberries. Try combining red, yellow, amber, and black raspberries for a spectacular presentation.

Strawberry Snow Pea Salad

PREPARATION: 15 MINUTES.
SERVES 6.

1 large head romaine lettuce
36 snow peas, ends and strings
  removed

2 cups strawberries, cut in half
raspberry vinaigrette dressing
  (page 65)

Wash romaine and remove any damaged leaves. Dry. Pull leaves apart. Select leaves for a salad bowl base. Blanch snow peas. Plunge in ice water to stop the cooking. Cook and dry. Arrange romaine leaves on 6 salad plates. Put snow peas on romaine in the form of a circle. Place a mound of strawberries in the center of each salad. Drizzle with raspberry vinaigrette.

The wild strawberry is sometimes called the beach strawberry.

Cape Cod Cranapple Salad

PREPARATION: 30 MINUTES.
SERVES 6–8.

2 cups fresh cranberries
1 cup water
½ cup sugar
3 tablespoons frozen orange juice
  concentrate, undiluted

1 apple, cored and coarsely
  chopped
½ cup walnuts, chopped

In a medium saucepan, cook cranberries in water over medium-low heat until they pop open, about 10–20 minutes. Add sugar and stir to dissolve. Remove and transfer to medium bowl and allow to cool. Add orange juice concentrate, apple, and walnuts. Refrigerate at least 1 hour before serving.

Raspberry Ribbon Salad

PREPARATION: 15 MINUTES.
SERVES 8–9.

2 3-ounce packages raspberry-
flavored gelatin
1½ cups boiling water
2½ cups raspberries
1 8-ounce bottle pitted Queen
Anne cherries, drained

1 8-ounce can mandarin oranges,
drained
1 banana, sliced
1 cup sour cream

Dissolve gelatin in boiling water. Add raspberries. Stir in banana, cherries, and oranges. Pour half mixture in 8-inch square pan and refrigerate 30 minutes or until gelatin begins to sit. Spread sour cream over gelatin. Top with remaining gelatin mixture. Refrigerate until firm.

Blueberry-Orange Olive Salad

PREPARATION: 35 MINUTES.
SERVES: 4.

2 cups blueberries
6 tablespoons blueberry vinegar
(page 139)

2 teaspoons sugar
4 oranges, peeled and thinly sliced
1 cup black olives

Place the strawberries in a bowl with the vinegar and sugar. Let marinate at room temperature for about 30 minutes. Arrange orange slices on a serving plate or bowl and spoon the berries, without the vinegar, on top. Scatter the olives on top and then pour the vinegar over the salad. Serve cold.

Wild blueberries and huckleberries are very similar in appearance and flavor. The blueberry is a *vaccinium* and the huckleberry a *gaylussacia*—the blueberry has many small seeds and the huckleberry has ten hard (noticeable) seeds.

Strawberries and Champagne Ring

PREPARATION: 30 MINUTES.
SERVES 10–12.

Layer One:

2 envelopes unflavored gelatin
2 cups cold water
¼ cup sugar

1 6-ounce can frozen lemonade
  concentrate, undiluted
½ cup champagne

Layer One: Sprinkle the gelatin over *1 cup* of the cold water in a medium saucepan. Place over low heat, stirring constantly until the gelatin dissolves, about 3 minutes. Remove from heat. Add sugar and stir until dissolved. Add the frozen lemonade concentrate, stir until melted. Add the remaining 1 cup of water and the champagne. Pour into a 12-cup oiled mold and chill until almost firm.

Cream Layer:

1¾ cups cold water
½ cup sugar
2 6-ounce cans frozen lemonade
  concentrate, undiluted

1 cup champagne
2 cups heavy cream, whipped
1 quart strawberries, sliced in half

Cream Layer: Sprinkle the gelatin over the cold water in a medium saucepan. Place over low heat, stirring constantly until the gelatin dissolves. Remove from heat. Add the sugar and stir until dissolved. Add the frozen lemonade concentrate, stir un-

The gardeners of Henry VIII were the first to cultivate wild strawberries. Perhaps Henry was the first to woo a land with strawberries and cream. Strawberry leaves symbolize the rank of duke.

It's the Berries!

til melted. Add the champagne. Chill, stirring occasionally, until mixture is the consistency of unbeaten egg white. Fold in the whipped cream. Turn into the mold with the almost firm, clear gelatin mixture. Chill until firm. Unmold onto the serving platter. Serve with heaping portions of sliced strawberries.

Blueberry Lobster Salad

PREPARATION: 20 MINUTES.
SERVES 4.

2 cups cooked lobster meat, cut in chunks
2 tablespoons blueberry vinegar (page 139)
¼ teaspoon dry mustard
½ teaspoon salt
1 egg
1 cup olive oil
¼ cup blueberry yogurt
3 cups blueberries
3 kiwifruit, peeled and cut in chunks
1 cucumber, peeled and cut in chunks

The mellow flavor of the blueberry makes it a favorite of the young and old. The toddler loves to pick up these round, deep blue-colored balls, one by one; the teen feasts on blueberry pie a la mode; and the senior citizen breakfasts on a bowl of berries swimming in cream. Blueberries need no peeling or pitting; rinse and they are ready to be used in so many ways.

Chill lobster. In a blender or food processor mix vinegar, mustard, salt, and egg. Add oil slowly in a thin stream. After mayonnaise thickens, blend in blueberry yogurt. Toss lobster, blueberries, kiwifruit, and cucumber together. Pour dressing over. Refrigerate at least 2 hours before serving. Serve on a bed of red leaf lettuce.

Chinese Fruit Salad

PREPARATION: 15 MINUTES.
MAKES 12 SERVINGS.

2 cups mandarin oranges
1 pineapple, cut in 1-inch pieces
1 honeydew melon, scooped in
   balls

1 pint strawberries

Toss fruit together, then toss with dressing.

Orange Dressing:

¼ cup vegetable oil
¼ cup strawberry jelly
3 tablespoons strawberry vinegar
   (page 142)

¼ teaspoon salt

In a small bowl or jar, blend together dressing ingredients.

Mixed Fruit Salad

PREPARATION: 15 MINUTES.
SERVES 6.

2 cups blueberries or strawberries, halved
1 cantaloupe, cut in small squares

2 kiwifruit, peeled and sliced
salad greens of choice

Mix all fruit together and mound on greens.

Easy Poppyseed Dressing:

¾ cup oil
¼ cup blueberry vinegar (page 139)

1 teaspoon poppyseeds
½ teaspoon salt
1 teaspoon honey

In a small bowl or jar, blend dressing ingredients. Drizzle dress-ing over fruit and greens.

The strawberry is a member of the rose family. It is more widely esteemed for its flavor than any other fruit. It is the most common fruit grown in home gardens. Strawber-ries will grow almost every-where throughout the world, need little room to multiply themselves by producing "daughter plants," bear no thorns, need no trellises or supports. They can produce good crops without spraying because they bear fruit before pests get a good start.

Fruit Salad Combos

For a quick nutritious salad, served on a bed of greens, with your favorite dressing, try these tantalizing combinations:
• Pineapple chunks, strawberries, and walnuts
• Slices of red apple, avocado, and blueberries
• Half cantaloupe filled with crabmeat and blueberries, fruit salad dressing
• Honeydew balls, cantaloupe balls, red seedless grapes, and kiwifruit chunks on spinach
• Pineapple rings, mashed bananas mounded in the center of the ring and raspberry puree over top
• Plums, raspberries, and nectarines with a splash of raspberry vinegar, honey, and cinnamon
• Radishes, kiwifruit, tomatoes, and currants with half yogurt, half raspberry mayonnaise.
• Raw mushrooms, kiwifruit, and bean sprouts
• Grated carrots, cabbage, red seedless grapes, and blueberries
• Green and red pepper chunks, snow peas, and strawberries

Cranberry-Strawberry Yogurt Dressing

PREPARATION: 5 MINUTES.
MAKES 1 SCANT CUP.

½ cup strawberry yogurt   ¼ cup mayonnaise
3 tablespoons frozen cranberry
   juice concentrate, undiluted

Blend all together. Excellent on cold poultry.

The Jujeberry is sometimes called the blueberry of the Northern Plains. It has a higher vitamin C content than most citrus fruits. It tastes something like a combination of cranberries and blueberries. The fruit is small and apple-shaped.

Raspberry Walnut Vinaigrette

PREPARATION: 10 MINUTES.
MAKES 4–6.

¼ cup raspberry vinegar (page 140)
2 tablespoons shallots, minced
2 tablespoons parsley, minced

¼ cup walnuts, chopped
½ cup walnut oil
¼ cup vegetable oil

Combine vinegar, shallots, parsley, walnuts, salt, and pepper. Add walnut and salad oil in a steady stream. This dressing is also good with cold chicken.

Nagoonberries and wine berries resemble small raspberries and grow in Alaska and the Rockies.

Raspberry Mayonnaise

PREPARATION: 10 MINUTES.
MAKES 2 CUPS.

1 egg
1 teaspoon prepared mustard
1 teaspoon salt
dash cayenne pepper

2 tablespoons lemon juice
1½ cups salad oil
1 cup raspberries

Combine all ingredients in a blender but the oil and raspberries, and blend. With machine running, gradually add oil in a thin stream. Add raspberries a few at a time flicking the machine on and off. This mayonnaise is not a smooth consistency.

Blueberry Mustard Vinaigrette

PREPARATION: 5 MINUTES.
MAKES ½ CUP.

1 teaspoon Dijon-style, grainy or
  herb-flavored mustard
3 tablespoons olive oil

2 tablespoons blueberry vinegar
  (page 139)
salt and pepper to taste

Whisk together all the ingredients and serve.

5 Side Dishes

*E*ver try and convince a young child that green vegetables are delicious? Broccoli, green beans, and peas are all shunned, snubbed, and dismissed.

Chris, my youngest brother, cunningly slipped Brussel Sprouts to Daisey (the family Labrador) under the table wrapped in a napkin, one by one. By the end of the meal, there were usually three or four frayed napkins near his chair.

In this chapter, you'll find some new and wild vegetable and berry duos sure to turn the tastebuds of the most stubborn. We've included a few sophisticated dishes for special occasions.

Currant Glazed Parsnips

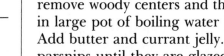

PREPARATION: 40 MINUTES.
SERVES 6.

1 pound parsnips	1 teaspoon salt
1½ cups water	½ teaspoon pepper
2 tablespoons butter	4 tablespoons currant jelly

Scrape outer skin with a potato scraper. Slice in quarters and remove woody centers and then slice into sticks. Cook parsnips in large pot of boiling water 30–35 minutes, until tender. Drain. Add butter and currant jelly. Salt and pepper. Keep turning parsnips until they are glazed.

Chefs regard currants as the rubies of their art. Used to add sparkle and color to fruit sauce or glaze. Currant glaze is used to make red patterns on pastries.

Cranberry and Pineapple Casserole

PREPARATION: 15 MINUTES.
BAKE 15 MINUTES.
SERVES 8.

2 cups cranberries, rinsed
½ cup pineapple juice
1 pound light brown sugar, packed

juice of 1 lemon
8 pineapple rings

Preheat oven to 375°F. Cook the cranberries, covered, in the pineapple juice until soft. Mash or puree in the blender, then sieve out the skins. Add sugar and lemon juice. Put the pineapple rings in a greased baking dish and add the puree to the top. Bake in preheated oven. Serve hot. This dish should be tart. It is excellent with ham or game.

Green Beans and Cranberry Puree

PREPARATION: 25 MINUTES.
SERVES 8.

1 cup water
1½ teaspoons salt, divided
1½ pounds green beans
½ cup light brown sugar, packed
½ cup orange juice
½ cup dry red wine

4 cups cranberries
½ teaspoon dried thyme, crumbled
¼ teaspoon ground pepper
2 tablespoons butter
½ cup blanched slivered almonds; reserve

In a large saucepan over high heat, bring water and 1 teaspoon salt to a boil. Cook beans in boiling water just until tender, about

When summer ends, here is an interesting Cranberry Skin Bleach to get rid of a fading tan. Take a handful of chopped cranberries and mix with some buttermilk. Spread on face. Lie down and keep mixture in place with a cloth. Leave on 20 minutes. Wash off with lukewarm water. Apply moisturizer.

5 minutes; drain and keep warm. In medium-sized saucepan, combine brown sugar, orange juice, wine, cranberries, ½ teaspoon salt, thyme, and pepper. Over medium heat cook until berries pop and sauce thickens slightly, about 10 minutes. In blender or food processor fitted with steel blade, puree cranberries until smooth; keep warm. In small skillet over medium heat, melt butter. Brown almonds in butter until golden brown. To serve, spoon puree over cooked beans and sprinkle with browned almonds.

Cranberry Stuffing

PREPARATION: 15 MINUTES.
MAKES 10 CUPS OF STUFFING.

1 12–13 pound turkey	1 teaspoon cinnamon
1 cup butter	1 teaspoon nutmeg
2 cups onions, chopped	2 teaspoons lemon rind
2 cups celery, chopped	2 teaspoons orange rind
2 cups cranberries	2 teaspoons poultry seasoning
1 cup dried currants	18 cups white bread cubes
1 teaspoon salt	3 eggs, slightly beaten

In a large pot, melt butter. Cook celery and onions until tender. Chop cranberries coarsely in food processor or blender. Add all ingredients and mix well with eggs. You will need 1 cup of stuffing per pound of bird. Do not stuff bird until ready to cook.

Lingonberries, or lowbush cranberries, grow in Alaska. They are national favorites in Sweden.

Cranberry Rice Croquettes

PREPARATION: 25 MINUTES.
MAKES 6 SERVINGS.

1 16-ounce can cranberry sauce,
   cut in cubes
3 tablespoons butter or margarine
3 tablespoons flour
½ teaspoon salt

1 cup milk
1½ cups cooked rice
fine dry bread crumbs
1 egg, slightly beaten

Melt butter, blend in flour and salt, add milk and cook until thick, stirring constantly. Add cooked rice. Spread on plate to cool. Coat rice mixture around sides of cranberry cubes forming balls. Roll in bread crumbs, egg mixture, and bread crumbs again. Fry in deep fat at 375°F until brown and crunchy. Drain on paper towels.

Cranberry juice has long been a popular beverage in New England, but only since 1967 has it been promoted as "cranberry cocktail" in the rest of the United States, by the largest producer, Ocean Spray, Inc.

Cranberry-Orange Butternut Squash

PREPARATION: 10 MINUTES.
BAKE 1 HOUR TOTAL.
SERVES 4.

2 butternut squash
3 tablespoons butter
3 tablespoons dark brown sugar

3 tablespoons orange marmalade
1 cup cranberries, rinsed and
   chopped

Preheat oven to 350°F. Split squash. Remove seeds. Place cut sides down on a baking dish. Bake 30 minutes. In a saucepan, melt butter. Stir in sugar, marmalade, and cranberries. Cook on low heat 5 minutes. Turn squash over and add cranberry mixture to the well in each squash. Bake another 30 minutes.

Cranberry, Wild Rice, and Sausage Stuffing

PREPARATION: 1 HOUR 15 MINUTES.
MAKES 4 CUPS.

½ pound wild rice
2 tablespoons butter
1 cup, onions finely chopped
2 Italian-style sweet fennel
 sausages

1½ cups cranberries
salt and freshly ground pepper to
 taste

Lingonberry is a type of cranberry and is known for a better flavor than the larger cranberry.

Place the wild rice in a saucepan and pour boiling water over it. Set aside, covered, for 1 hour. Then drain the rice, add fresh boiling water to cover by ½ inch. Bring to a simmer and cook gently until the rice is soft but not mushy. Drain well and set aside. Melt the butter in a sauté pan and gently cook the chopped onions until they are soft. Remove the skins from the sausages and add the sausage meat to the pan with the onions. Raise the heat slightly and cook, crumbling the sausage with a fork, until it is browned. Remove from the heat and add the wild rice to the mixture. Mix well. Rinse the cranberries. Chop them roughly or process them briefly in a food processor or blender. Add to the sausage-rice mixture and mix well. Taste for seasoning, and add salt and pepper if necessary.

Gingered Snow Peas, Blackberries, and Apples

PREPARATION: 10 MINUTES.
SERVES 4.

2 tablespoons freshly grated
   ginger
2 tablespoons corn oil for frying

2 cups snow peas
1 large Granny Smith apple, sliced
2 cups blackberries

In a skillet, sauté ginger in oil. Add snow peas and apple until "crunchy." Just before serving, toss in blackberries.

Spinach with Currants and Pine Nuts

PREPARATION: 15 MINUTES.
SERVES 4–6.

2 pounds fresh spinach, washed
   (may substitute 2 pounds broccoli, coarsely chopped)
2 tablespoons unsalted butter
3 tablespoons olive oil
1 teaspoon fresh garlic, finely
   chopped
¼ teaspoon finely ground white
   pepper

¼ cup fresh currants (or dried and
   "plumped" by soaking overnight in fruit juice or Cassis)
4 tablespoons pine nuts (pignolis)
3 tablespoons freshly grated
   Parmesan cheese
1 tablespoon unsalted butter,
   melted

Place spinach in a large pot, sprinkle with a little water, cover, and cook over high heat until wilted, turn leaves occasionally.

One of the theories used by scientists to support the belief that North America and Europe were once one land mass, is the fact that wild blackberries are native to both continents. The distance across the Atlantic Ocean is too great for the seeds to have been carried by winds or birds.

Drain through a colander, pressing down with back of saucer to remove excess moisture. Chop spinach coarsely. Heat butter and oil in deep, heavy pot. Add garlic and pepper, and cook over low heat 1 minute. Add currants and pine nuts and cook over low heat 1 minute. Add spinach or broccoli and mix well. Place vegetable mixture on gratin dish or shallow heatproof serving dish. Sprinkle grated cheese and melted butter on top. Brown under hot broiler. This recipe can be assembled in a serving dish a few hours ahead; then rewarmed in 300°F oven.

Indian Rice

PREPARATION: 15 MINUTES.
BAKE 1 HOUR.
SERVES 4–6.

1 Spanish onion, finely chopped
1 tablespoon safflower oil
1½ cups long grain brown rice
1 egg, beaten
¼ teaspoon freshly ground white pepper
1 tablespoon saffron mixed with 2 tablespoons hot water
3 cups chicken stock

¼ cup soy sauce
½ teaspoon ground cardamom
2 tablespoons blanched split almonds
¼ cup currants, "plumped" in hot water ½ hour
1 tablespoon orange zest, grated
1 tablespoon lemon zest, grated

Preheat oven to 350°F. In small sauté pan, cook onion in oil until translucent. Set onion aside. In deep, heavy pot (1½ quart) mix rice with egg. Stir over moderate heat until kernels are dry and separate. Season with pepper. Add onion, saffron, stock, and soy sauce. Stir over moderate heat until liquid comes to a brisk boil. Add cardamom, almonds, currants, orange and lemon zests. Stir mixture. Cover with firm-fitting lid and bake in preheated oven. When cooked, fluff rice with 2 forks. Cooked rice can be packed into a lightly greased mold and turned on to a warm plate or simply piled into a warm serving bowl.

Cranberry Leek Compote

PREPARATION: 50 MINUTES.
SERVES 4–6.

½ cup currants
2 tablespoons apple cider,
   unsweetened
4 cups cranberries, rinsed and
   sorted
1 cup apple cider, unsweetened

1 cup sugar
6 tablespoons butter
2¼ pounds leeks (white and light
   green parts), sliced
salt and freshly ground pepper to
   taste

Soak currants in 2 tablespoons apple cider for 30 minutes to "plump." Heat cranberries, cider, and sugar in saucepan over low heat, stirring occasionally, until sugar dissolves. Increase heat to a boil then reduce heat and simmer until berries pop, about 7 minutes. Set aside. Melt butter in heavy large skillet over medium-low heat. Add leeks and cook until soft and beginning to color, stirring frequently, about 25 minutes. Season with salt and pepper. Add currants and their soaking liquid. Increase heat and bring to boil. Add cranberry mixture. Reduce heat and simmer 5 minutes to blend flavors, stirring occasionally. Adjust seasoning. Cool. Can be prepared 5 days ahead. Cover and refrigerate. Best served at room temperature.

6 Breads & Breakfast Fare

Each blueberry may encase as many as 65 palatable seeds. These seeds do not detract from its juicy texture. The surface of the berry has a dusty, silvery appearance that is a natural wax coating, protecting the berry from too much sun. If blueberry picking in the Lake Huron area, look for arrowheads as well as berries. Indians in this region gathered and dried blueberries in the sun for later use with meats and in soups. Blueberries grow on bushes that can reach 15 feet in height and bear fruit from May through September.

*U*ntil the end of the eighteenth century, yeast or spirits were used to raise breads, or air was beaten into the dough along with eggs. In the 1790s, Pearlash—a refined form of potash that produces carbon dioxide in dough—was discovered.

In the 1850s, baking powder was commercially produced, saving homemakers a good deal of time preparing rolls, biscuits, muffins, griddle cakes, and tea breads.

Quick bread recipes are ideal for berries. Quick breads use baking powder or soda as leavening agents and do not require the proofing or rising time of yeast bread. The "quick" preparation and cooking time is easy on the fruit and the cook. And the results? What more rousing aroma than the scent of home-baked muffins or the sound of fresh blueberry pancakes on the grill? Here are brunch crowd pleasers, lazy day Sunday breakfast pleasures, and easy ideas for simple breakfasts in a flash.

Blueberry Sour Cream Pancakes

PREPARATION: APPROXIMATELY 20 MINUTES.
MAKES 18 PANCAKES ABOUT 3 INCHES IN DIAMETER.

1⅓ cups flour (unsifted)
½ teaspoon baking soda
1 teaspoon salt
1 tablespoon brown sugar
½ teaspoon nutmeg

1 tablespoon cinnamon
1 egg, beaten
1 cup sour cream
1 cup whole or skim milk
1 cup blueberries, rinsed

Stir the flour, soda, salt, sugar, nutmeg, and cinnamon together thoroughly. Combine the egg, sour cream, and milk, and add to the dry ingredients, stirring just enough to combine. Add the blueberries carefully, blending them just enough to mix in the berries. Drop the batter by a ¼ cupful onto a hot, greased griddle. Cook until the surface is covered with bubbles; turn and cook until the other side is well browned.

Blackberry Gingerbread Waffles

PREPARATION: 15 MINUTES.
SERVES 6.

2 cups flour
3 teaspoons baking powder
1½ teaspoons powdered ginger
3 eggs

4 tablespoons butter, melted
1 cup buttermilk
4 tablespoons molasses
½ cup blackberries

Preheat waffle iron. In a large bowl, mix flour, baking powder, ginger. In a separate bowl, beat eggs, butter, buttermilk, and

Blackberry winter is an English term for a cold early May when blackberries first come into bloom. Blackberry summer is a period of fine weather in late September and early October.

molasses. Mix ingredients together just enough to moisten. Fold in berries. Pour mixture onto seasoned waffle iron and cook until steam no longer rises.

Blueberry Cinnamon Doughnuts

PREPARATION: 30 MINUTES.
MAKES 30 DOUGHNUTS.

2 eggs
1 cup sugar
1 cup buttermilk
4 cups white flour
1 teaspoon baking powder
½ teaspoon baking soda
½ teaspoon salt

½ teaspoon nutmeg
2 teaspoons cinnamon
2 tablespoons butter, melted
½ cup blueberries, rinsed
frying oil heated to 365° F
2 teaspoons cinnamon
½ cup sugar

Beat eggs, sugar, and buttermilk together. Sift flour, baking powder, soda, salt, nutmeg, and cinnamon together; stir into the egg mixture. Add melted butter. Fold in blueberries. Roll or pat out dough on a floured board to ½ inch thick. Using a well-floured cutter, cut shapes and allow them to rest on a floured surface 5 minutes. Heat enough fat or oil to fill 3 inches of a frying kettle. When oil is 365° F, drop in a piece of doughnut to test. Drop in 3 or 4 doughnuts. As soon as they float to the surface and hold their shape, turn them. Fry until golden on both sides (approximately 3 minutes). Drain on absorbent paper. Combine cinnamon and sugar and sprinkle on doughnuts while warm (best when eaten immediately).

Blackberry tea (made from the leaves, stems, and berries) was known as a sure cure for dysentery. During the Civil War, truces were called when both armies needed to go "blackberrying."

Currant Cassis Scones

PREPARATION: 30 MINUTES.
BAKE 14 MINUTES.
MAKES 12 SCONES.

¾ cup dried currants
⅓ cup Cassis
2 cups sifted unbleached all-purpose flour
1 tablespoon baking powder
¼ teaspoon salt
⅓ cup sugar

1 teaspoon grated lemon peel
6 tablespoons unsalted butter, chopped, room temperature
1 egg, beaten to blend
¾ cup half-and-half
melted butter
sugar

Preheat oven to 450°F. Combine currants and Cassis in heavy small saucepan and bring to boil, stirring constantly. Cover and let stand overnight, stirring occasionally. Position rack in center of preheated oven. Sift flour, baking powder, and salt into medium bowl. Mix in sugar and peel. Cut in butter until mixture resembles coarse meal. Drain currants; stir into mixture. Make well in center. Place egg in measuring cup. Blend in enough half-and-half to equal ¾ cup. Add to well. Stir just until dough comes together. Turn out onto well-floured surface and knead gently just until dough holds together, about 12 times. Cut dough into 3 pieces. Gently pat each piece into a ¾-inch-thick round. Cut each round into quarters, pushing straight down with floured sharp knife. Arrange on ungreased baking sheet, spacing ½ inch apart. Brush tops with melted butter and sprinkle with sugar. Bake in preheated oven. Cool for 5 minutes on rack before serving.

Deep garnet red raspberries are the base for the liqueur *Crème de Framboise*. The raspberry's intense flavor is a favorite throughout Europe.

Sour Cream Raspberry Coffee Cake

PREPARATION: 20 MINUTES.
BAKE 20 MINUTES.
SERVES 6–8.

1½ cups flour
1 cup sugar
2 teaspoons baking powder
½ teaspoon baking soda
¼ teaspoon salt

1 cup sour cream
2 eggs, lightly beaten
1 cup raspberries
1 cup coconut

Preheat oven to 350°F. Grease and lightly flour a 9-inch square baking pan. In a medium bowl, combine flour, sugar, baking powder, baking soda, and salt. In a small bowl, beat sour cream and eggs. Pour into flour mixture and beat until smooth. Fold in raspberries and coconut. Spread mixture into prepared pan.

Crumb Topping:

¼ cup flour
¼ cup butter
½ cup brown sugar, packed

1 teaspoon cinnamon
½ cup coconut

In a separate bowl, toss all topping ingredients with a fork to combine. Sprinkle crumb topping over batter. Bake in preheated oven. Cool slightly before cutting. Serve warm.

Fanny Heath, a determined pioneer woman who landed in North Dakota, had been warned that she could grow nothing on her barren alkaline soil. After 40 years of hard labor, her homestead blossomed with fruit and vegetables. After her death in 1931, the black raspberry she developed was named in her honor.

Strawberry Fritters

PREPARATION: 20 MINUTES.
SERVES 4–6.

1 jar apricot preserves
2 pints fresh strawberries, hulled
  and rinsed
2 cups ground or grated filberts
  or walnuts

2 eggs, slightly beaten
2 cups cracker crumbs
peanut oil heated to 365° F

Force preserves through sieve. Dip each strawberry in apricot liquid fully. Allow excess to drip off. Coat berry with ground nut crumbs. Dip in beaten eggs. Coat with cracker crumbs. Place on wire rack for at least 30 minutes to set coatings. Fry at 365° F a few at a time. Drain on toweling and serve warm with confectioner's sugar.

New York state became the center for strawberries in the 1800s. Albany's horticulturist, James Wilson, developed the hardy Wilson variety. In the 1880s, 100,000 acres were being cultivated. Refrigerated cars meant the perishable berry could be held and shipped to the Midwest.

Boysenberry Whole Wheat Muffins

PREPARATION: 20 MINUTES.
BAKE 25–30 MINUTES.
MAKES 12 MUFFINS.

6 tablespoons butter or margarine
¾ cup honey
2 eggs
2 cups whole wheat flour

4 teaspoons baking powder
½ cup milk
2 teaspoons cinnamon
2 cups fresh boysenberries

Preheat oven to 375°F. Grease 12 muffin cups or line with paper liners. Cream butter or margarine and honey; add eggs and beat well. Combine dry ingredients and add to batter alternately with milk. Crush ½ cup berries and add to batter by hand, then fold in rest of berries. Fill prepared muffin cups very full. Bake in preheated oven. Cool before removing from pan.

Blueberry-Lemon Muffins

PREPARATION: 15 MINUTES.
BAKE 15–20 MINUTES.
MAKES 12 MUFFINS.

2 cups all-purpose flour
⅓ cup sugar
2½ teaspoons baking powder
½ teaspoon salt
1 egg, beaten

grated rind of 1 lemon
½ cup lemon juice
¼ cup plus 1 tablespoon milk
¼ cup salad oil
½ cup blueberries

Preheat oven to 400° F. Grease bottoms of 12 muffin cups or line with paper liners. In a large bowl, mix flour, sugar, baking powder, and salt. In a small bowl, mix remaining ingredients except berries. Form a well in flour mixture and add egg mixture all at once. Stir just until flour is moistened (avoid over mixing). Gently fold in blueberries. Spoon batter into prepared muffin cups. Bake in preheated oven. Remove from pan and cool on wire rack.

The early settlers used blueberries in white wash to paint their houses gray.

Strawberry Streusel Muffins

PREPARATION: 20 MINUTES.
BAKE 20–25 MINUTES.
MAKES 12 MUFFINS.

1½ cups flour
½ cups sugar
2 teaspoons baking powder
¼ teaspoon salt
1 egg, lightly beaten

½ cup unsalted butter
½ cup milk
1 teaspoon almond extract
1 cup strawberries, sliced

Preheat oven to 350° F. Line 12 muffin cups with paper liners. In a medium bowl, combine flour, sugar, baking powder, and salt. Make a well in the center. In a separate bowl, beat egg, butter, milk, and extract. Add to dry ingredients all at once and stir until just combined. **Do Not Overmix.** Fill each muffin cup ¾ full with batter.

Streusel Topping:

½ cup chopped toasted almonds
½ cup sugar
¼ cup all-purpose flour

2 tablespoons unsalted butter, melted
⅛ teaspoon almond extract

To make topping, combine all topping ingredients into one bowl. Sprinkle evenly over the top of each muffin. Bake in preheated oven.

Strawberry Nut Bread

PREPARATION: 25 MINUTES.
BAKE 45 MINUTES.
MAKES 2 LOAVES.

In 1624, Francis Bacon wrote, "the strawberry wives laid two or three great strawberries at the wide mouth of the pot, and all the rest were little ones." Buyers must still beware.

2 cups all-purpose flour
1 teaspoon baking soda
½ teaspoon salt
¾ cup sugar
½ cup butter, softened

2 eggs
2 teaspoons almond extract
1 cup plain yogurt
1 cup chopped almonds
2 cups strawberries

Preheat oven to 350°F. Grease and flour two 7⅜ by 3⅝-inch loaf pans. In a small bowl, thoroughly stir together flour, baking soda, salt; set aside. In a large bowl, cream sugar and butter. Add eggs and almond extract and beat until fluffy. Add flour mixture and yogurt alternately to creamed mixture, beating until blended after each addition. Fold in chopped nuts first, then strawberries. Turn batter into 2 prepared pans. Bake in preheated oven. While still warm, glaze with Almond Glaze. Cool in pans. Remove from pans and keep in refrigerator.

Almond Glaze:

1 cup sifted powdered sugar
1 teaspoon almond extract

2–3 tablespoons milk

Combine sifted sugar, almond extract, and enough milk for drizzling. Drizzle on loaf while warm.

Very Lemon-Blueberry Bread

PREPARATION: 25 MINUTES.
BAKE 1 HOUR, 10 MINUTES.
MAKES 1 LOAF.

⅓ cup butter, melted
1 cup granulated sugar
3 tablespoons fresh lemon juice
2 eggs
1½ cups sifted flour
1 teaspoon baking powder

1 teaspoon salt
½ cup milk
2 tablespoons grated lemon rind
½ cup chopped walnuts (optional)
1 cup blueberries, tossed with
 flour to coat

Preheat oven to 350°F. Grease and flour 9 by 5 by 3-inch loaf pan. In a large bowl, mix the butter, cut sugar and lemon juice. Beat in the egg. In another bowl, sift together flour, baking powder, and salt. Add the flour mixture to the butter mixture alternately with the milk, stirring just enough to blend. Stir in blueberries, grated rind, and nuts. Pour the batter into the greased and floured loaf pan. Bake in preheated oven. Baking time will vary depending on the wetness of the berries. Cool 10 minutes. Remove the bread from the pan and while still warm, drizzle lemon glaze over the top and into the cracks that form while baking. Store, foil wrapped for 1 day before slicing.

Fruit picked for freezing should be slightly underripe. For making jam and jelly, fruit should be slightly overripe.

Lemon Glaze:

¼ cup lemon juice   ½ cup granulated sugar

In a small bowl, combine the lemon juice and sugar. Mix well.

It's the Berries!

Classic Strawberry Yeast Bread

PREPARATION: 2 HOURS, 20 MINUTES.
BAKE 35–40 MINUTES.
MAKES 2 LOAVES.

Strawberries. The subject of many myths—the Greeks had a taboo against eating red foods, thus many believed that the wild strawberry possessed great powers. The plant began to be cultivated in Europe in the Middle Ages. Pregnant women avoided strawberries because they believed their children would be born with strawberry birthmarks. Strawberries were considered a medicinal cure for anything from colds to gum disease.

2 packages dry yeast
½ cup warm water
1 cup milk, scalded
2 eggs, beaten
1 teaspoon salt

¼ cup sugar
4 tablespoons butter, melted
1 cup strawberries
1 tablespoon lemon juice
5–5½ cups flour

Preheat oven to 375°F. Grease two 8½ by 4½ by 2½-inch loaf pans. Dissolve yeast in warm water. Set aside. In mixing bowl, combine milk, eggs, salt, sugar, and butter. Mix well. Stir in strawberries and lemon juice. Gradually add flour and beat well after each addition. When you have added enough flour to make dough firm, knead on a floured surface for 8–10 minutes. Place in greased bowl. Cover and let rise until doubled in bulk (about 1 hour). Punch down and let rise to double again (about 1 hour). Dough is ready if when pressed with finger, impression remains. Divide into 2 loaves. Place in greased bread pans and bake in preheated oven.

Montana Huckleberry Corn Bread

PREPARATION: 15 MINUTES.
BAKE 35 MINUTES.
MAKES 6–8 WEDGES.

⅓ cup cornmeal
⅓ cup whole wheat flour
⅓ cup wheat germ
3 teaspoons baking powder
2 eggs, slightly beaten

¼ cup vegetable oil
¼ cup honey
1 cup buttermilk
1 cup huckleberries

Preheat oven to 350°F. Grease 9-inch round cake pan. Combine cornmeal, flour, wheat germ, and baking powder. Make a well in center. In a separate bowl, mix eggs, oil, honey, and buttermilk. Add to dry ingredients all at once. Blend until just moistened. Fold in huckleberries. Pour into prepared pan. Bake in preheated oven.

Huckleberries were so little, plentiful, and common a fruit that "a huckleberry," in the early 1800s, became slang for an inconsequential person. This term probably inspired Mark Twain to name his hero Huckleberry Finn.

The huckleberry's commonness and abundance were immortalized in such colloquial phrases as "thick as huckleberries," and "to get the huckleberry," or to be ridiculed. To be "a huckleberry to someone's persimmon" meant to be nothing in comparison with something else. To be "a huckleberry over someone's persimmon" meant to outrank someone.

Cranberry-Applesauce Oat Bread

PREPARATION: 20 MINUTES.
BAKE 50–60 MINUTES.
MAKES 1 LOAF.

½ cup butter, softened
½ cup light brown sugar, packed
½ cup honey
2 eggs
1 cup applesauce
¾ cup all-purpose flour, sifted
1½ teaspoons baking powder

1 teaspoon baking soda
1 teaspoon cinnamon
1 teaspoon nutmeg
1 teaspoon cloves
1 cup rolled oats
1 cup fresh cranberries, rinsed

Preheat oven to 350°F. Grease and flour 9 by 5 by 3-inch loaf pan. In a medium bowl, cream butter and sugar. Beat in honey, eggs, and applesauce. Mix together the dry ingredients. Stir into the applesauce mixture. Stir in cranberries and oats. Fill greased and floured baking pan. Bake in preheated oven. Cool 10 minutes, then remove from loaf pan and continue to cool.

Huckleberry Oatmeal Muffins

PREPARATION: 15 MINUTES.
BAKE 20–25 MINUTES.
MAKES 12 MUFFINS.

1 egg
⅓ cup sugar
3 tablespoons butter, melted
1 cup milk
1 cup oatmeal

1 cup flour
1 tablespoon baking powder
1 teaspoon salt
1 cup huckleberries, rinsed (tossed in flour)

Preheat oven to 400° F. Grease bottoms of 12 muffin cups or line with paper liners. In a large bowl, beat egg, sugar, butter, and milk. In a large bowl, combine dry ingredients. Combine wet and dry ingredients until moistened; batter should be lumpy. Fold in huckleberries. Spoon batter into prepared muffin cups ⅔ full. Bake in preheated oven. Remove immediately from pan and cool on wire rack.

7 Desserts

My grandparents' summer home on the New Jersey shore was the family hub each August. Sunday suppers drew cousins, friends, and neighbors round the heavy oak table set with linen and china to the one formal meal of the week.

Everyone's favorite dessert was plump blueberries, fresh from the farmers' market and laced with heavy cream (delivered each morning in thick squat bottles).

As the evening faded and the ocean mist cooled, a soft breeze fluttered summer curtains. We children learned to sit quietly with the grown-ups at the table, slowly finishing the sweet fruit and cream that soothed our sunchapped lips as we savored the last of a summer's day.

Mulberry Macaroon Ambrosia

PREPARATION: 10 MINUTES.
SERVES 4–6.

4–5 cups mulberries, rinsed
1 cup sugar

1 cup crumbled macaroon cookies
½ cup blanched, ground almonds

In a medium saucepan, cook mulberries with sugar over low heat until juices are released. In a separate bowl, combine cookie crumbs and almonds. Gently fold in mulberries. Divide between dessert bowls and chill. Serve with whipped cream.

"Mulberry Mania," of the 1830s echoed California's Gold Rush for get-rich-quick schemes on the East Coast. Following the example of two Connecticut brothers who cultivated silkworms from mulberry trees, farmers across Connecticut, New Jersey, Pennsylvania, and Ohio turned their fields into mulberry nurseries. Societies devoted to silk were formed. Prices spiraled then, but when trees glutted the market, a "mulberry blight" struck. Groves died. "Mulberry Mania" plummeted to an end.

Blueberry-Orange Tart

PREPARATION: 20 MINUTES.
BAKE 20 MINUTES.
MAKES 1 TART.

1 cup orange juice
¼ cup freshly grated orange peel
½ cup butter
1 cup sugar
6 eggs, slightly beaten

9-inch partially baked tart crust
(page 116)
2 cups fresh blueberries, rinsed,
and sorted

Preheat oven to 400°F. In a medium bowl, whisk orange juice, grated orange peel, and melted butter. Beat in eggs and sugar. Pour mixture into partially baked shell. Bake in preheated oven. Place blueberries over warm filling. Press them in lightly with the back of a spoon. Dust with confectioner's sugar when cool.

Huckleberry Pie (The true "Fly Pie")

PREPARATION: 10 MINUTES.
BAKE 50–60 MINUTES.
MAKES 1 PIE.

1 basic pie 9-inch crust (page
116)
3 cups huckleberries
¾ cup sugar

3 tablespoons minute or instant
tapioca
2 tablespoons butter

Preheat oven to 400°F. Prepare pie crust dough. Roll out dough to ⅛ inch thick. Ease into a 9-inch pie tin. Roll out remaining dough and set aside. Toss huckleberries with sugar and tapioca.

The Little Red Schoolhouse, an inn in Lakeside, Montana specializes in homemade Fly Pie and Silver Dollar Huckleberry Pancakes. This recipe for Fly Pie was cajoled from the baker, a student on summer break. Fly pie is a standard "valley" pastry.

Turn berry mixture into crust. Dot with butter. Ease top crust over filling. Trim and crimp edges. Cut slits in top to allow steam to escape. Bake in preheated oven.

Cranberry-Walnut Bread Pudding

PREPARATION: 25 MINUTES.
BAKE 30 MINUTES.
SERVES 4–6.

2 cups cranberries
1¼ cups brown sugar, divided and packed
1 cup walnut pieces
2 tablespoons grated orange rind
1 tablespoon Cointreau
8 slices white bread, crusts removed

4 tablespoons butter, softened
1 cup milk
1 cup heavy cream
½ cup orange juice
3 eggs, lightly beaten

Preheat oven to 350°F. In a food processor or blender, chop cranberries. Add ¾ *cup* brown sugar, walnuts, orange rind, and Cointreau, process until just combined. Spread mixture in an 8-inch square baking pan. Spread bread with butter. Arrange buttered side down in 2 layers over mixture. In a small bowl, whisk together milk, cream, orange juice, and remaining brown sugar and eggs. Pour evenly over cranberry mixture. Let mixture stand loosely covered at room temperature at least 1 hour or overnight in refrigerator. Put baking pan in larger pan. Add enough hot water to larger pan to reach halfway up sides of 8-inch pan. Bake in preheated oven. Let pudding cool in water bath 5 minutes. Serve pudding warm with whipped cream.

Cranberry-Apple Brown Betty

PREPARATION: 15 MINUTES.
BAKE 15–20 MINUTES.
SERVES 6.

1 cup cranberries, rinsed and
 sorted
2 apples peeled, cored, and sliced
1 tablespoon lemon juice
3 cups dry bread crumbs

½ cup butter, melted
1¼ cups sugar
1 teaspoon cinnamon
1 teaspoon nutmeg

Preheat oven to 375°F. Butter a 2-quart baking dish. In a medium bowl, combine cranberries, apples, and lemon juice. In a separate bowl, toss bread crumbs, butter, sugar, and spices. Assemble the Betty in layers. Sprinkle ⅓ bread crumb mixture into baking dish, follow with ⅓ apple-cranberry mixture. Repeat twice more. Bake in preheated oven.

No one knows who Betty was, the originator of the first Apple Brown Betty. The dish was first mentioned in print in 1864. Every version has its own special personality attached to it. This one was a favorite of my aunt, who helped me bake it when I spent the night at her home—my very first "pie."

Blueberry Grunt

PREPARATION: 30 MINUTES.
SERVES 6.

1 tablespoon cornstarch
½ cup water
2 cups blueberries
½ cup sugar
¼ teaspoon cinnamon

1 cup flour
1¼ teaspoons baking powder
¼ teaspoon salt
1 egg, well beaten
¼ cup milk

In a medium saucepan, dissolve cornstarch in water, add blueberries and bring to a boil. Let simmer 3 minutes while com-

pleting the remaining steps. In a medium-sized bowl, sift dry ingredients. In a separate bowl, combine egg and milk and then add to dry ingredients. Stir to moisten. Drop dough by large spoonsful on the boiling berries. Allow space between dumplings to expand. Cook covered for 15 minutes. Serve warm with whipped cream or ice cream.

Anyberry Mousse

PREPARATION: 45 MINUTES.
SERVES 4.

4–6 cups berries (strawberries, blueberries, raspberries, blackberries, alone or in any combination)
2 tablespoons fresh lemon juice

1 tablespoon unflavored gelatin
6 tablespoons boiling water
2 egg yolks
⅔ cup granulated sugar
2 cups heavy cream, chilled

In a blender or food processor, combine berries, lemon juice, and gelatin. Puree until smooth. Pour in boiling water, process again. Set aside. In the top part of a double boiler, beat egg yolks with sugar until pale yellow and thick. Set over simmering water and stir until slightly thick. Cool to room temperature. Combine egg mixture and berry mixture. Chill until just beginning to set. In a small bowl, whip cream until stiff. Fold cream into berry mixture. Spoon into individual serving glasses or serving bowl. Chill at least 4 hours, garnish with whole berries just before serving. This makes a delicious pie served in a graham cracker, ginger snap, or chocolate cookie crust.

Blueberry Grunt is also called "Blueberry Slump" because this somewhat misshapen dish slumps on the plate, causing the cook to grunt!

Peach Melba with Raspberry Sauce

PREPARATION: 30 MINUTES.
SERVES 4.

4 fresh peaches
1 cup sugar
1 cup water

1-inch vanilla bean
1 cup raspberry sauce (page 127)
vanilla ice cream

Peel and halve peaches. In a medium saucepan, combine sugar and water and add vanilla bean. Bring to a boil, cook 5 minutes. Lower heat to simmer, add fruit, poach gently, basting with hot liquid. When tender (not too soft) remove pan from heat and allow to cook in syrup. Then chill. When very cold, arrange on a scoop of vanilla ice cream and coat with raspberry sauce.

This dessert was created by Chef Georges Auguste Escoffier (1846–1935) and named for the Australian opera singer Nellie Melba (1859–1930). The dish has become a favorite in American dining rooms.

White Chocolate Mousse with Blackberries

PREPARATION: 35 MINUTES.
MAKES 1 GENEROUS QUART.

9 ounces good quality white chocolate, chopped
¾ cup milk
1½ cups whipping cream
3 egg whites

¼ teaspoon cream of tartar
1 teaspoon vanilla
1 cup blackberries, rinsed (raspberries may be substituted)

Melt chocolate in double boiler over low heat. Warm milk and cream, whisk into chocolate until smooth. Cool. Beat egg whites with cream of tartar until they hold soft peaks. Fold into chocolate mixture, being careful not to overmix. Pour this mixture over whipped cream. Add vanilla. Fold in blackberries. Pour into sherbet glasses or a glass bowl. Garnish with blackberries and chill.

Pavlova

PREPARATION: 30 MINUTES.
BAKE 1–1¼ HOURS.
SERVES 4.

Pavlova was created by an Australian chef when the famous ballerina visited Sydney in the 1930s. It is a lovely, light, and delicate dessert.

4 egg whites, room temperature
¼ teaspoon salt
¼ teaspoon cream of tartar
1 cup fine granulated sugar
4 teaspoons cornstarch
1 teaspoon vanilla extract

1 cup chilled whipping cream
2–3 cups mixed fresh berries
2 medium kiwifruit, peeled and
  chopped
sugar to taste

Preheat oven to 275°F. In a medium bowl, beat egg whites, salt, and cream of tartar until they hold stiff peaks. Add sugar slowly while beating. Beat in cornstarch and vanilla. Butter an 8-inch cake pan or pie tin and fill with meringue mixture, spread higher around the edges. Bake in preheated oven. Cool slightly. Unmold, slide onto a serving plate and finish cooling completely. Whip cream. Gently cut a circle 2 inches in from edge of meringue and pry off top. Fill shell with cream and fruit and replace "lid." Serve immediately.

Strawberry Shortcake with Strawberry Whipped Cream

PREPARATION: 25 MINUTES.
BAKE 12–15 MINUTES.
MAKES APPROXIMATELY 5½ CUPS.
SERVES 6–8.

1¾ cups sifted all-purpose flour
½ teaspoon salt
1 tablespoon sugar
3 teaspoons baking powder
6 tablespoons butter
¾ cup milk (or cream for a richer cake)

1 quart (or more) strawberries, rinsed, hulled, and sliced
strawberry whipped cream (see recipe below)

Preheat oven to 450°F. In a large bowl, cut butter into dry ingredients. Make a well in the center and add milk all at once. Stir until the dough is free from sides of bowl. Turn onto lightly floured board. Knead gently, making about 10 folds. Roll with a lightly floured rolling pin until dough is ¼ inch thick. Cut with a biscuit cutter dipped in flour. Brush tops with melted butter. Place on ungreased baking sheet and bake in preheated oven. Makes 12 3-inch round shortcakes. Split shortcakes while hot and spread with butter. Top with sliced strawberries, whipped cream, and then biscuit top. Garnish with whipped cream.

Berries and cream, whether liquid, clotted, sour or frozen, make a perfect marriage. The sweet smooth texture of the cream counter balances the sharp sweetness of the berry.

Strawberry Whipped Cream

2 cups fresh strawberries, hulled
  and rinsed
2 tablespoons confectioner's sugar

1 teaspoon vanilla
2 cups whipping cream

In food processor or blender, puree strawberries with confectioner's sugar. Whip cream with sugar and vanilla in chilled bowl until stiff (about 3–4 minutes). Gently fold ¼ of cream into strawberry puree, then fold mixture back into remaining cream. Refrigerate. Strawberry cream can be prepared up to 1 hour ahead. May substitute 1 8-ounce container non-dairy topping for whipped cream.

The colonists invented strawberry shortcake. The largest strawberry shortcake is baked each year at the annual Lebanon, Oregon Strawberry Festival—a huge cake towering over 12 feet in the air is cut with a two-person saw.

THE TRADITION OF STRAWBERRY SHORTCAKE

Truly an American concoction, strawberry shortcakes vary as widely as do strawberry growing regions. Most often the shortcake is made of rich biscuit dough, baked to flaky perfection. This is split in half and slathered with butter. The lower layer is heaped with berries, sprinkled with sugar, and capped with the biscuit top, which in turn is topped with more berries and sugar. The whole is then served with a pitcher of cream.

In old Nantucket kitchens, a strawberry shortcake is made with a rich egg bread. In the South, raspberries and peaches make a delicious filling, capped off with meringue topping. In New Hampshire, blueberry-apple shortcake is sweetened with maple syrup.

Strawberries Romanoff

PREPARATION: 20 MINUTES.
SERVES 4–6.

4 cups strawberries
1 tablespoon granulated sugar
1 cup vanilla ice cream
1 cup heavy cream

1 tablespoon fresh lemon juice
2 tablespoons Cointreau
mint sprigs for garnish

In a large bowl, combine berries and sugar. In a separate bowl, whip the ice cream until soft. In a medium bowl, whip the heavy cream until stiff and fold into the ice cream. Add lemon juice and Cointreau. Pour mixture over berries and stir gently. Pour into individual serving glasses and serve immediately. Garnish with fresh mint.

Coeur à La Crème with Strawberries

PREPARATION: 20 MINUTES.
SERVES 2–4.

1 pound cottage cheese (not low fat or diet)
8 ounces cream cheese
½ cup sour cream
2 tablespoons confectioner's sugar

½ heavy or whipping cream
fresh strawberry dessert sauce (page 128)
1 pint fresh whole strawberries, rinsed and hulled

Coeur A' La Crème, cream heart, is a classic French dessert that makes a pretty presentation when decked with strawberries—an elegant St. Valentine's Day dessert.

Combine cottage cheese, cream cheese, and sour cream in a medium bowl with electric beaters. Beat on high 1 minute or until smooth and creamy. Add confectioner's sugar. In a separate

bowl, whip the heavy cream. Fold cream into cheese mixture. Line a 3-cup heart mold (or sieve or colander) with cheesecloth. Allow the cloth to hang over the edges. Spoon mixture into the lined container. Fold the cheesecloth over the top and place the mold on a bowl, or deep plate, and store in refrigerator 8 hours or overnight. To serve, spoon half the strawberry sauce onto a platter. Invert mold and remove cheesecloth. Garnish with fresh strawberries.

White chocolate is not chocolate at all but a blend of whole milk and sugar cooked until condensed to a solid state. Sometimes cocoa butter is added for the chocolate flavor; if not, artificial flavor is used. Its creamy smooth texture and mild taste complement delicate berries.

Chocolate or White Chocolate Dipped Strawberries

PREPARATION: 20 MINUTES.
MAKES 24 STRAWBERRIES.

½ pound white, dark, or milk chocolate

24 whole strawberries with stems

Line a baking sheet with waxed paper. Melt chocolate in double boiler over simmering water. Holding each strawberry by stem, dip into chocolate and place on waxed paper. Allow to dry in a cool spot. Drizzle white chocolate over chocolate-dipped strawberries. Drizzle dark or milk chocolate over white chocolate-dipped strawberries. These make elegant garnishes, simple desserts, and lovely hostess gifts.

Berry Fool

PREPARATION: 20 MINUTES.
SERVES 8.

4 cups gooseberries, strawberries, blackberries, or raspberries
1 cup sugar (depending on berries' sweetness)

¼ cup water
2 cups heavy cream

In a medium saucepan, combine berries with sugar and water.
Cook over low heat until tender, stirring frequently and pressing down with fork to extract juices. Puree mixture in food processor or blender. Strain to remove seeds if desired. Chill mixture.
Just prior to serving, whip cream until stiff peaks form. Fold into
berry mixture. Spoon into serving bowl or glasses. Garnish with
additional berries.

Gooseberry Fool

According to British cookbook author, Jane Grigson, a fool is "a
word that goes with trifle and whim-wham (trifle without the
custard)—names of nonsensical bits of folly, *jux d' esprit,* outside
the serious range of cooking repertoire. The kind of thing that
women are said to favour, but that men eat more of."[1] From
Kettner's Book of the Table (1877), author E. S. Dallas gives the
following instructions for a gooseberry fool:

"Scald gooseberries sufficiently with a very little water till all
the fruit breaks—when the gooseberries are cold, mix them all
together. Passing them through a sieve or colander spoils them.

The gooseberry has nothing to
do with the goose—and is
the result of a combination of
old English and French
names, garbled over the years.
In France, it is known as the
mackerel currant because it
goes so well with oily food.

The fine natural flavor which resides in the skin no art can replace. The skins must therefore remain unseparated in the general mash. Sweeten with fine powdered sugar, but add no nutmeg or other spice. Mix in at the last moment some rich cream, and it is ready. The young folks of North Hamptonshire, after eating as much as they possibly can of this gooseberry fool, are said frequently to roll down a hill and begin eating again."[2]

[1]Grigson, Jane. *Jane Grigson's Fruit Book*. New York: Atheneum, 1982.
[2]Ibid.

Frozen Amaretto Soufflé with Blueberries

PREPARATION: 25 MINUTES.
MAKES 3 PINTS.

<table>
<tr><td>5 egg yolks</td><td>¼ cup amaretto</td></tr>
<tr><td>¾ cup sugar</td><td>½ cup toasted almonds, chopped</td></tr>
<tr><td>3 cups whipping cream</td><td>1 cup blueberries</td></tr>
</table>

In a small bowl, beat yolks and sugar. In a separate bowl, beat cream to hold stiff peaks. Add amaretto. Fold in egg mixture with blueberries and almonds. Butter sides of a 1-quart soufflé dish. Cut a waxed paper lining to form a collar that will stand at least 1 inch above the rim of the dish. Clip collar together with paper clip. Fill soufflé ½ inch above the rim and freeze. Before serving, remove collar and let soufflé stand 10–15 minutes to soften. Garnish with fresh berries and toasted almonds.

The word *soufflé* means "breath" in French.

Cookie Tulips with Fresh Strawberries

PREPARATION: 35 MINUTES.
BAKE 5–7 MINUTES.
SERVES 4–6 (16 COOKIES).

5½ tablespoons butter
½ cup sugar
½ teaspoon vanilla extract

3 egg whites
½ cup plus 2 tablespoons flour
½ teaspoon cornstarch

Preheat oven to 375°F. Generously butter and lightly flour 2 cookie sheets. In a medium bowl, cream butter with sugar and vanilla until light and fluffy. Slowly add egg whites. Fold in flour and cornstarch. Batter should be smooth. With a tablespoon, drop dough onto cookie sheet and using a spatula, spread dough into a 6-inch circle. Allow about 2 inches between each cookie. Bake in preheated oven. Remove with a long spatula and place over upturned custard cup or cup with no handle. Press edges of cookie down lightly to form tulip shape. Leave about 20 seconds or until cookies will hold shape.

Strawberry Filling:

2 pints fresh strawberries, hulled
and rinsed

1 cup raspberry puree (page 122
see Anyberry Dessert Purees)

Place a tablespoon of puree on individual dessert dishes. Place tulip cookie on top of each plate. Fill with fresh strawberries and drizzle with raspberry puree.

Roger Williams, who founded Providence, Rhode Island in 1636 wrote, "The strawberry is the wonder of all fruit growing naturally in those parts—I have many times seen as many as would fill a good ship. The Indians bruise them in a Morter, and mix them with meal and make Strawberry Bread."

It's the Berries!

Kiwifruit-Hazelnut Meringue Cake

PREPARATION: 45 MINUTES.
BAKE 3 HOURS TOTAL.
SERVES 8.

1 cup hazelnuts	¾ cup sugar
3 egg whites	

Preheat oven to 300°F. Toast hazelnuts under a broiler 3–4 minutes. Rub with a clean cloth to remove skins. Discard skins. Place nuts in a blender or food processor and chop very finely. In a medium bowl, beat egg whites until stiff, add *half* the sugar, and beat until smooth. Carefully fold in remaining sugar and hazelnuts. Cover baking tray with parchment paper or lightly buttered aluminum foil and make 3 even circles of meringue mixture, about 7 inches in diameter. (One circle may have to be cooked on another tray.) Bake in preheated oven for 1 hour reducing temperature to 225°F for 2 hours. Cook until dry and crisp. Layers may be stored in an airtight container.

Kiwifruit Filling:

4–5 kiwifruit, peeled	1 tablespoon confectioner's sugar
1 cup whipping cream	1 tablespoon Cointreau

Peel kiwifruit, halve lengthwise, and slice across. Whip cream and sugar until stiff, fold in liqueur. Spread ¼ of the cream on top of the 1 layer of meringue cake—add a few slices of kiwifruit. Top with another layer of meringue, spread with more cream and fruit. Place top layer of cake on top; spread with remaining cream and decorate with kiwifruit slices.

Kiwifruit is really a Chinese gooseberry. It was renamed when New Zealand fruit traders realized that they would have difficulty selling a "Chinese gooseberry," in American ports. They renamed it kiwi, in honor of the tiny fuzzy New Zealand bird.

Vermont Maple Cream

PREPARATION: 40 MINUTES.
SERVES 4–6.

2 cups milk (or for richer cream,
   combination of milk and cream)
1 cup maple syrup

2 tablespoons cornstarch
dash salt
2 eggs, beaten

In the top of double boiler, scald 1¾ cups milk with maple syrup. Combine the remaining milk with cornstarch and salt, add to milk stirring constantly. Cook over medium heat 25 minutes. Add 2 tablespoons of maple-milk mixture to beaten eggs and whisk. Add egg mixture to pan slowly, stirring constantly 5 minutes. Pour into serving dish. Chill and serve over any berry combination.

Anyberry Sorbets

PREPARATION: 20 MINUTES.
MAKES 1 QUART.

4 cups berries (strawberry, blueberry, cranberry, raspberry, or
   black raspberry)

¾ cup sugar (depending on sweetness of fruit—cranberries may
   require more, blueberries may
   require less)
⅓ cup fruit juice

In a food processor or blender, puree the fruit. Strain seeds from puree. In a saucepan, combine the sugar and fruit juice and stir over low heat until sugar is dissolved. Add fruit puree and stir to combine. Pour into an 8-inch square pan and place in

Huckleberries with crackers and cream—an old colonial recipe. In a bowl, put two soda crackers, broken; add some berries, sugar, and cold heavy cream.

2 large Stalks Rhubarb diced. & cooked on medium w/ 1/4 cup water until done. Col Slightly add 1/2 cup honey. instead of Sugar & Juice.

It's the Berries!

the freezer. Stir every 15 minutes or until creamy. Cover and freeze. Scoop into serving dishes and garnish with mint sprigs. If you have an ice cream maker, follow manufacturer's directions.

Candied Cranberries

PREPARATION: 25 MINUTES.
MAKES ½ CUP (APPROXIMATELY 50 BERRIES).

½ cup firm cranberries, rinsed   ½ cup sugar
½ cup water

Wash and dry berries and prick each with a needle. Boil sugar and water until syrup spins thread (234°F). Add berries. Cook until syrup forms hard ball in cold water. Lift berries from syrup. Place on waxed paper. Let stand until dry. Roll in granulated sugar. Use like cherries. Store in tightly sealed jars.

Minted Berry Toss

PREPARATION: 5 MINUTES.
SERVES 4–6.

¼ cup fresh lemon juice   4 cups berries or combination ber-
¼ cup fresh mint   ries and fresh fruit
2 tablespoons sugar or to taste

Combine in a medium bowl and toss in berries with sliced fresh fruit. Chill before serving.

Berry-Cassis White Chocolate Cheesecake

PREPARATION: 40 MINUTES.
BAKE 50–55 MINUTES TOTAL.
MAKES 1 CHEESECAKE.

1 vanilla crumb crust (page 116)
   prepared and put into a 9-inch
   pan

1 pint fresh raspberries, strawberries, blueberries, blackberries,
   loganberries, or kiwifruit,
   rinsed and peeled

Filling:

2 8-ounce packages cream cheese,
   room temperature
1 cup sugar
4 ounces grated white chocolate
   (about ¾ cup)

4 tablespoons Cassis
4 large eggs

Preheat oven to 350°F. In a large bowl, mix cream cheese with sugar. Add white chocolate and Cassis until well blended. Beat in eggs, one at a time and continue beating until smooth. Pour filling into prepared crust. Bake 40–45 minutes. Remove and place on a rack to cool. Keep oven on.

America is the only country in the world to cultivate blackberries. It wasn't until the 1830s that they were cultivated in the states. Many considered them a nuisance or a weed. Sometimes they were used for medicinal purposes. It was, finally, listed in cookbooks as an alternate fruit to be used in some recipes and gradually became quite popular.

Topping:

1 pint (2 cups) sour cream
¼ cup sugar

1 teaspoon vanilla extract

In a small bowl, combine ¼ cup sugar, vanilla, and sour cream until well blended. Pour over slightly cooled cheesecake. Return cheesecake to oven and bake the additional 10 minutes. Place cheesecake on rack and allow to cool. Arrange berries decoratively around top. Cover cheesecake with foil and refrigerate at least 12 hours before serving. Cheesecake will be soft.

The gooseberry is a very welcome sign in England—it heralds the coming of spring and summer and more berries.

Zabaglione

PREPARATION: 20 MINUTES.
SERVES 4.

6 egg yolks
3 tablespoons sugar

⅔ cup marsala

In the top part of a double boiler, whisk egg yolks with sugar over simmering water until thick and creamy. Add marsala and beat with whisk until mixture thickens to triple in volume. Serve over fresh berries. This Italian sauce may be served warm or chilled. If chilled it will lose some volume.

Basic Pie and Tart Crust

PREPARATION: 30 MINUTES.
BAKE 20 MINUTES.
MAKES 1 8- OR 9-INCH CRUST.

1 cup flour
½ teaspoon salt
⅓ cup plus 1 tablespoon vegetable
   shortening

2–3 tablespoons water

Preheat oven to 425°F. In a medium bowl, combine flour and salt. Cut in shortening. Sprinkle in water, 1 tablespoon at a time, mixing until all flour is moistened and dough cleans side of bowl. Gather dough into ball; shape into a flattened round on lightly floured board. With flour dusted rolling pin, roll dough out about 2–2½ inches larger than pie or tart pan. To place in pan, fold into quarters. Then place in pan and unfold. Prick dough all over with fork. Bake unfilled pie or tart crust in preheated oven.

Vanilla Crumb Crust

PREPARATION: 10 MINUTES.
MAKES 1 9-INCH CRUST.

2 cups vanilla wafers
¼ cup sugar

½ cup butter, melted

In a medium bowl, combine crumbs, sugar, and butter with a fork. Press into pie plate or spring mold.

116

It's the Berries!

8 Sweet Berry Preserves

*O*ur first year in Minnesota, winter hit hard and early with a blizzard in mid-November and temperatures of -10°F for two full weeks. New Jersey and my mother's kitchen seemed planets away. Short on friends and long on time, I was determined to make Christmas presents for the family back home.

I mentioned my project to a neighbor one evening as we stood in line at the grocery store check-out. It was something she'd always wanted to do and we decided to collaborate that Sunday, sharing recipes and ingredients. Leslie brought tiny, wild strawberries she had picked near her family's cabin in Bayfield, Wisconsin in July and frozen. My freezer was stocked with huckleberries brought back on the plane from Flathead Valley, Montana.

These November Sundays are a nine-year tradition, a holiday salute to a very close friendship.

Preserve Definitions

Jam:
Fruit jam is sweetened, concentrated fruit pulp. It is one of the easiest methods of preserving fruit.

Jelly:
Fruit jelly is cooked, strained, reduced, and sweetened fruit pulp.

Kiwifruit cannot be used in gelatins. The enzyme, *actindin*, in the fruit stops the jelling process.

Marmalades:
Once made exclusively with citrus fruit, marmalade originally took its name from the marmelo quince, a hard astringent fruit when fresh, but a soft sweet preserve.

Preserves:
Fruit, preserved through continuous poaching in sweetened syrup—preserves were often served at royal banquet tables in sixteenth century England.

Conserves:
Fruit conserves are like preserves, with the addition of nuts and dried fruit. They are delicious on ice cream, crackers, and toast.

Fruit Butter:
Fruit butters are purees that have been reduced through cooking into thick, rich spreads. Fruit butters contain little sugar but lots of flavor.

Curds:
Rich fruit custard curds are made of pureed fruit, eggs, and butter. They make delicious spreads and fillings for tarts and pies.

Syrups:
Presweetened fruit essences have been cooked and strained. Syrups are delicious on pancakes, ice cream, or with a splash of club soda on ice.

Purees:
Made of berries that are sweetened and mashed, purees add color and flavor to pudding, cakes, and ice cream. Fresh berry purees are deliciously simple.

How to Sterilize and Process Jars

If you plan to keep preserves without refrigeration, it is essential to pack them in sterilized jars. There are a variety available on the market—hardware stores, supermarkets, houseware shops, and through the mail. Be sure to read and follow jar manufacturer's instructions, but here are a few basic guidelines.

To sterilize jars and lids. Wash jars and lids in hot soapy water and rinse. Place in a large kettle filled with boiling water to cover. Boil 5 minutes, remove kettle from heat and let jars stand in hot water until ready to use.

Just before filling, remove jars and lids with tongs and invert on towels to drain. Fill the jars, wipe rims clean with a warm, damp towel and fasten lids securely. Place in large deep kettle (preferably one with a wire rack on the bottom). Pour enough boiling water into the kettle to cover jar by 3 inches. Boil jars for 10 minutes. Remove from kettle and allow to cool at room temperature. Store in a cool dry cupboard. Refrigerate immediately after opening.

Pots for Preserving. It's best to use a 4–5-quart saucepan that is deeper than it is wide with a lid. It should also not be much wider than the cooking burner on your range. The best materials are ceramic-coated cast iron, or coated aluminum. (Untreated aluminum causes a harmless chemical reaction between the pot and its contents.)

Tips for Preserving the Season

Use only the best fruit—berries at the peak of their ripeness or substitute frozen. Frozen berries will exhude more juice because freezing and thawing have damaged the cell structure. Allow an additional 5–10 minutes cooking time to reduce juices when using frozen berries.

Pectin is the substance that helps make jellies, jams, and preserves jell. Some berries contain more pectin than others. Fruit low in pectin must be combined with high pectin fruit or with commercial pectin to make jelly.

Berries high in pectin: blackberries, cranberries, raspberries
Berries with good pectin level: boysenberries, loganberries
Berries low in pectin: blueberries, kiwifruit, strawberries

Old-Fashioned Elderberry Jelly

PREPARATION: 25 MINUTES.
MAKES ABOUT 4 HALF-PINT JARS.

8–9 pints (16–18 cups) elder-berries, rinsed sugar	2 tablespoons fresh lemon juice

In a large pot, cook berries over low heat for 15 minutes, covered, then 10 minutes uncovered. Stir and crush berries against the side of the pan. Strain berry mash through a fine sieve or a colander lined with cheesecloth for 3 hours. Measure berry juice and pour into heavy large pan. Measure out amount of sugar equal to berry juice and set aside. Bring berry juice to boil. Add sugar to pot, ½ cup at a time, allowing liquid to return to the boil before adding more. Add lemon juice after first cup of sugar has been added. Boil liquid about 12 minutes or until it

Elderberries were known as "magic berries" because the bark, leaves, and fruit were renown for their medicinal properties. They induce labor and aid digestion.

The wood of the elderberry tree is white, hard, and close-grained. It has been used to make a variety of articles including skewers, combs, shoemaker's pegs, whistles, popguns, and other toys. The sap has been used to make insect repellent and the flowers have been used in lotions and perfumes.

passes the jelly test, or reaches 220°F on a candy thermometer. Skim jelly, ladle into hot sterilized jars and process according to manufacturer's directions.

Quick Mint-Currant Jelly

PREPARATION: 5 MINUTES.
MAKES 1 CUP.

2 teaspoons fresh mint leaves, chopped

½ teaspoon grated orange rind
1 cup or 6-ounce jar currant jelly

Remove currant jelly from jar, and place all ingredients in top of a double boiler. Stir gently until well blended. Pour jelly back into glass and cover. Refrigerate 24 hours. You can use the same method with any herb combined with any jam, jelly, or honey.

THE JELLY TEST
HOW TO TELL WHEN IT'S "JELLY"

1. Cold Plate Test: Mixture will wrinkle on a cold plate if it has jelled.
2. Spoon Test: Mixture will fall in a single sheet from a spoon.
3. Thermometer Test: A candy thermometer will read 220°F at sea level.

Anyberry Dessert Purees

PREPARATION: 10 MINUTES.
MAKES 1¼–1½ CUPS.

2–3 cups berries
¼ cup fruit liqueur

¼–½ cup sugar or to taste

In a small saucepan, combine all ingredients and stir to mash berries. Warm over low heat to dissolve sugar. Transfer to food processor or blender and puree. Strain if desired. Berry purees are fabulous drizzled over yogurt, pudding, custard, fruit salad, lady fingers, pancakes, and crêpes.

Wild Blackberry Syrup

PREPARATION: 20 MINUTES.
MAKES 4 PINTS.

2 quarts (8 cups) ripe blackberries
2½ pounds sugar
1 3-inch piece stick cinnamon

1½ tablespoons whole cloves
1 cup brandy

Mash berries and strain to extract juice. Measure 2 pints juice. In large kettle, combine 2 pints juice, sugar, and spices. Simmer gently 15 minutes. Cool. Strain syrup through several layers of cheesecloth. Add brandy to strained syrup. Mix well. Bottle in attractive containers and cap or cork. If a thicker syrup is desired, cook an additional 10 minutes before adding brandy.

DYNAMIC DUOS

Strawberry-Amaretto
Raspberry-Cassis
Blueberry-Chambord
Blackberry-Cointreau
Black Raspberry-Peach
  Tree Schnapps
Boysenberry-Kir
Cranberry-Apple Barrel
  Schnapps

Cranberry-Tangerine Conserve

PREPARATION: 20 MINUTES.
MAKES 3–4 HALF-PINT JARS.

2 tangerines
½ cup water
½ cup sugar
1 pound cranberries (4 cups)

2 cups water
2 cups sugar
½ cup pecans

Cut tangerines into small pieces and remove seeds, do not peel. In a small saucepan, combine tangerines with ½ cup water and ½ cup sugar and simmer over low heat until soft. Set aside. Cook cranberries in 2 cups water. Add 2 cups sugar and continue cooking until mixture thickens. Add tangerine mixture and nuts to cranberry mixture. Ladle into hot sterilized jars and seal according to manufacturer's instructions.

Low-Calorie Berry Puree

PREPARATION: 5 MINUTES.
MAKES 1½ CUPS (47 CALORIES PER ¼ CUP SERVING).

3 cups berries (strawberries, black-
    berries, raspberries, kiwifruit,
    alone or in combination)

2 teaspoons honey
1 teaspoon lemon juice

Two cups of berries equal one cup of puree.

Place all ingredients in food processor or blender and puree. Strain and remove seeds if desired. Refrigerate. Willl keep up to 5 days.

Blackberry-Honey Jam

PREPARATION: 20 MINUTES.
MAKES 3 HALF-PINT JARS.

5 cups blackberries
1¼ cups honey

2 tablespoons lemon juice

In a large saucepan, combine blackberries and honey. Crush slightly. Let stand 20 minutes to release juices. Add lemon juice. Bring mixture to a boil over medium heat and cook 10–15 minutes or until thick. Ladle into hot sterilized canning jars. Process according to manufacturer's directions. Experiment with some of the different honeys available (clover, buckwheat).

Spiced Gooseberry Jam

PREPARATION: 20 MINUTES.
MAKES 7 HALF-PINT JARS.

4 cups gooseberries, blossom and
   stem ends removed
2 sticks cinnamon
10 cloves

3 whole allspice
6 cups sugar
1 3-ounce package liquid pectin

In a large saucepan, crush fruit with spoon and combine with spices and sugar. Cook over low heat. Bring to a boil over high heat, stirring constantly 1 minute. Remove from heat. Add liquid pectin. Skim jam. Ladle into hot sterilized jars and process according to manufacturer's directions.

Gooseberries were so commonly used in Elizabethan England, that Shakespeare used the expression, "not worth a gooseberry."

Boysenberry Curd

PREPARATION: 20 MINUTES.
MAKES 2 CUPS (ENOUGH FOR 1 9-INCH TART).

4 cups boysenberries
½ cup sugar
4 tablespoons unsalted butter

2 teaspoons lemon juice
2 eggs
2 egg yolks

In a food processor or blender, puree berries then strain to remove seeds. Pour mixture into medium saucepan and warm over low heat. Stir in sugar, butter, and lemon juice. Whisk together eggs and egg yolks, then whisk into berry mixture. Cook over low heat, stirring constantly until thick. It should reach 170°F on a thermometer. Chill mixture.

Boysenberries were named for botanist Rudolph Boysen who developed this hybrid from blackberry-raspberry stock in 1923.

Cranberry-Walnut and Butter Spread

PREPARATION: 5 MINUTES.
MAKES 1½ CUPS.

1 cup cranberries, rinsed
1¾ cups confectioner's sugar
½ cup butter

1 tablespoon orange juice
2 tablespoons walnuts

Combine cranberries and sugar in blender or food processor with a steel blade until pureed. Add butter and orange juice and process until smooth. Stir in walnuts. Transfer to a serving dish and chill 1 hour or until firm.

Raspberry-Almond Cream Cheese

PREPARATION: 5 MINUTES.
MAKES 1 CUP.

1 3½-ounce package cream cheese
1 cup raspberries
¼ cup confectioner's sugar

½ teaspoon almond extract
¼ cup toasted almonds

In a food processor fitted with a steel blade or a blender, process berries with cream cheese, sugar, and extract. Add almonds and turn into a small bowl and refrigerate until firm.

Fresh Cranberry-Ginger Sauce with Almonds

PREPARATION: 15 MINUTES.
MAKES APPROXIMATELY 3 CUPS.

1 pound fresh cranberries (approximately 4 cups), rinsed
1½ cups sugar
½–1 teaspoon ground ginger to taste

grated rind of 1 orange
juice of 1 orange
juice of ½ lime (optional)
½ cup coarsely slivered almonds

In a saucepan, combine all ingredients except the walnuts. Cover and bring to a boil. Reduce the heat and simmer until the cranberries split open, about 10 minutes. Set aside. Toast the almonds on a baking sheet in the oven for 10 minutes at 350°F. When cool, add them to the cranberry mixture. Chill before serving.

The mulberry tree has been romanticized throughout literature as the symbol of lost youth. It will not sprout leaves until spring is certain; they die with the first frost.

Fresh Raspberry Dessert Sauce

PREPARATION: 10 MINUTES.
MAKES 2½ CUPS.

2 tablespoons cornstarch
¼ cup Chambord, Cointreau, or
  port

4 cups raspberries
½ cup sugar

In a small saucepan, combine cornstarch and liqueur. Add raspberries and sugar. Stir over low heat until mixture simmers and thickens.

Blackberry-Ginger Preserves

PREPARATION: 45 MINUTES.
MAKES APPROXIMATELY 5 HALF-PINT JARS.

10–11 cups blackberries
3 tablespoons grated fresh ginger
½ cup orange juice

7 cups sugar
zest of 1 orange

In a large pot, place berries and gently mash with wooden spoon. Warm over low heat 15 minutes to extract juices. Add ginger and orange juice and gently warm over low heat. Bring mixture to a boil and add sugar ½ cup at a time stirring constantly. Add orange zest. Allow mixture to boil 10–20 minutes until it reaches 220°F on a candy thermometer or passes the jelly test. Remove from heat. Ladle into hot sterilized jars and process according to manufacturer's directions.

The royal raspberry belongs to the rose family. It grows all across Europe, Scandinavia, and Greece.

Fresh Strawberry Dessert Sauce

PREPARATION: 25 MINUTES.
MAKES 2½ CUPS.

1 quart (4 cups) fresh strawberries
1 cup sugar

2 tablespoons peach liqueur, kirsh,
or amaretto

Mash berries in medium saucepan. Add sugar and cook over low heat with sugar. Press mixture through a fine sieve. Add liqueur, chill. Can substitute raspberries for strawberries and serve over fresh strawberries.

Do not pick berries on rainy days as they will not keep well.

Cranberry-Apricot Butter

PREPARATION: 25 MINUTES.
MAKES 3 HALF-PINT JARS.

1 quart cranberries, rinsed
1 cup apricot nectar

1½ cups light brown sugar, packed
1 teaspoon cinnamon

Boil the cranberries in the nectar until very soft. Puree in the blender. Sieve to remove the skins. Put back on the stove with the sugar and cinnamon and cook until thick. This thickens more as it cools. Ladle into hot sterilized jars and process according to manufacturer's directions.

Cranberry-Orange Maple Sauce

PREPARATION: 25 MINUTES.
MAKES ABOUT 5 CUPS.

2 cups water
1 pound fresh cranberries (approx-
　imately 4 cups), rinsed
⅓ cup freshly squeezed orange juice

1½ cups maple syrup
2 tablespoons grated orange rind
1 teaspoon ground ginger or 2 ta-
　blespoons grated

In a large saucepan, combine ingredients and simmer 20 minutes stirring often until sauce is slightly thick.

Raspberry-Almond Conserve

PREPARATION: 50 MINUTES.
MAKES 6 HALF-PINT JARS.

3 pints (6 cups) cranberries
3 cups granulated sugar
2 tablespoons orange juice
2 tablespoons amaretto or
　Cointreau

1 cup almonds, toasted and
　coarsely chopped.

The raspberry may take its name from the English "to rasp" or scrape, referring to the thick raspberry bushes.

Combine all the ingredients except almonds in a heavy saucepan. Cook over low heat until sugar dissolves, about 5 minutes. Increase the heat and bring to a low boil. Cook for 30
minutes, stirring frequently. Remove from heat and stir in almonds. Pack immediately in hot sterilized jars and process according to manufacturer's directions.

9 Condiments

*B*efore refrigeration made fresh food a way of life, condiments were an expected part of each meal. As a child, I remember the side table in my mother's dining room where mustard and homemade relishes stood beside the silver cruet rack that held the vinegar, oil, salt, and pepper. A hot dog without relish is unthinkable! What is a hamburger without catsup? Certain foods are meant to marry, and that is what relishes and chutneys do.

Just as chutney was developed in India to mask the often spoiled meat, relishes were developed to use left-over, or aging foods in the root cellar and pantry.

Recently the culinary world has undergone a revived interest in fruit chutneys and berry relishes. Not long ago, while browsing in a gourmet shop, I noticed the price tag of a blueberry chutney was $7.50 and cranberry relish $4.25. The bottles and packaging were lovely, and perhaps so were the contents.

The recipes included in this chapter present chutneys and relishes that are easy to make in your own kitchen. So—why not stock your pantry and make some for friends? Both fresh and frozen fruit can be interchanged and the time spent is minimal in return for the pleasure you will get from your efforts.

The American strawberry originated in South America. It found its way to France by ship to the Royal Gardens and then to Brittany. The male and female plants were crossed accidentally and produced the "pineapple strawberry"—now the major cultivated berry today.

Condiment Definitions

Chutney:
A fruit relish of East Indian inspiration. Chutneys often accompany a variety of main dishes.

Relish:
Side dish savories—fruit relishes are often not cooked or only cooked slightly so fruit retains its shape.

Vinegars:
The darlings of the New American Cuisine—fruited vinegars are delightfully easy to make. They add an elegant touch to salads, sautés, even desserts.

Glazes:
The final step to add flavoring and decoration to a dish.

Sauces:
Special touches that can make a dish special.

Sweeten cranberries after they've cooked—cooking with sugar toughens the skins.

Cranlilli

PREPARATION: 25 MINUTES.
MAKES 1½ CUPS.

1 cup cranberries	½ cup sugar
1 medium onion, chopped	½ cup white wine vinegar
1 green pepper, diced	½ teaspoon salt

In a small saucepan, combine all ingredients and simmer over low heat covered, about 10 minutes. Uncover and simmer 10 minutes more. Serve chilled with meat or poultry.

Onion and Cassis Relish

PREPARATION: 35 MINUTES.
MAKES 1 CUP.

2 medium onions, sliced
1 cup Cassis
⅛ cup water
¼ cup dark brown sugar, packed

2 tablespoons red wine vinegar
4 black peppercorns
4 cloves
½ cup currants

Mix everything in a glass or enamel pot, except currants and bring to a fast boil. Reduce and simmer 30 minutes. Add currants. Cool. Adjust seasoning.

Kiwifruit Tomato Relish

PREPARATION: 35 MINUTES.
MAKES 3 HALF-PINT JARS.

8 tomatoes, peeled and coarsely chopped
8 kiwifruit, peeled and coarsely chopped
2 large onions, chopped
1 green pepper, seeded and chopped

1 yellow pepper, seeded and chopped
1½ cups honey
2 cups white wine vinegar

Simmer all ingredients in an enamel or glass pot for 30 minutes or until thick. Spoon into hot sterilized jars processed according to manufacturer's directions. Volume may vary due to size of products used.

The kiwifruit stores exceptionally well. It is picked hard and allowed to ripen slowly in a cool area while being shipped. The kiwifruit will store, when ripe, for up to six weeks in the refrigerator. Kiwifruit should be soft as a ripe pear for best eating.

Three Classic Cranberry Relishes

Fresh Cranberry Relish

PREPARATION: 5 MINUTES.
MAKES 3 CUPS.

2 cups cranberries   1½ cups sugar
2 oranges, cut in quarters and
    seeded (do not peel)

In a food processor or blender, combine cranberries, oranges,
and sugar until finely chopped. Keep covered in refrigerator.

Cranberry-Honey Relish

PREPARATION: 10 MINUTES.
MAKES 1¼ CUPS.

2 cups cranberries   ½ cup honey (or maple sugar, or
                                          combination of both)

In a small saucepan, cook cranberries in honey until skins pop.
Remove from stove and cool. Store in refrigerator.

The Indians mixed cranberries with dried venison for meat patties called *pemmican*. These were carried on hunting and exploring expeditions—the original beef jerky.

Cranberry-Apple Spice Relish

PREPARATION: 5 MINUTES
MAKES 2 CUPS.

2 cups cranberries
1 large Granny Smith (or other tart) apple

½ cup brown sugar, packed
½ teaspoon nutmeg

In a food processor or blender, process all ingredients to desired consistency. Refrigerate.

Blueberry Szechuan Sauce

PREPARATION: 15 MINUTES.
MAKES ABOUT 1 CUP.

½ cup frozen blueberry juice, diluted
¼ cup sherry
1 tablespoon cornstarch
¾ teaspoon salt
1 teaspoon crushed Szechuan pepper (available in Chinese market)

2 crushed Hunan peppers (available in Chinese market)
½ teaspoon grated fresh ginger
½ teaspoon lime juice
2 cloves of garlic, pressed

Combine all ingredients. Cook over medium heat until thick and clear. The flavors improve by standing. Use as dipping sauce for shrimp. Make ahead so flavors develop.

Blueberries are small round tart-packed treats. Blueberries cultivated for the market are sweet and large. Wild berries are small, heavily seeded, and intense in flavor. Both possess a deep blue color that adds to their beauty. The skin has a silver dusty appearance that is nature's wax coating that protects the berry from too much sunlight.

Strawberry-Mustard Horseradish Sauce

PREPARATION: 5 MINUTES.
MAKES ¾ CUP.

1 tablespoon prepared mustard
1 tablespoon strawberry juice,
    undiluted

1 teaspoon horseradish
4 strawberries, mashed

In a small bowl, combine all ingredients and mash with a fork. Good on white fish or chicken breasts.

Blueberry Relish

PREPARATION: 65 MINUTES.
MAKES 6 CUPS.

3 cups sugar
1¼ cups water
3 pints (9 cups) blueberries
1½ cups red wine vinegar
grated zest of 2 oranges

4 cinnamon sticks, broken
2 teaspoons whole allspice
1 teaspoon whole coriander seed
1 teaspoon whole cloves
1 teaspoon whole cardamom

In a large saucepan, combine sugar and water over medium heat. Bring to a slow boil and boil 1 minute. Add berries and return mixture to boil. Reduce heat to medium-low and cook mixture uncovered, 5 minutes. Remove from heat. Strain berries from syrup, reserving syrup. Set berries aside. Return syrup to pan. Add remaining ingredients. Boil mixture uncovered until reduced by half (about 50 minutes). Syrup will register 220°F

Bright red, succulent strawberries. A favorite berry in the United States—they are now grown as an industry in Arkansas, California, Florida, Louisiana, Michigan, and New Jersey, giving our supermarket shopper a good supply twelve months of the year.

on candy thermometer or pass jelly test (see p. 121). Add berries to mixture. Reduce heat to medium boil for 5 minutes. Ladle into hot sterilized jars and seal according to manufacturer's directions.

Blueberry Chutney

PREPARATION: 35 MINUTES.
MAKES 7–8 HALF-PINT JARS.

1 pound plums, pitted
4 cups red wine vinegar
1½ cups water
1⅓ cups onion, chopped
1½ cups red peppers, chopped
2 cloves of garlic, mashed
1 teaspoon salt
2 teaspoons dry mustard

3 teaspoons ground ginger
2 teaspoons orange zest
½ teaspoon cayenne pepper
2 teaspoons ground cloves
3 cups dark brown sugar, packed
4 cups blueberries
1 cup dried currants

Pit plums and cut in pieces. In a glass or enamel pot, combine vinegar, water, onions, peppers, garlic, salt, mustard, ginger, orange zest, cayenne pepper, and cloves. Simmer 15 minutes. Add sugar and plums. Simmer until it thickens. Stir gently so as not to break fruit. Add blueberries and currants and cook about 10 minutes. Seal in hot sterilized jars processed according to manufacturer's directions. Hold for a month before using to allow the flavors to marry.

Berries grown for market are picked, boxed, and sold according to pint measure. Ninety berries of the more expensive grade fill one box, whereas 190 of lesser grade will fill the same size box.

Vinegar

The sharp, acrid-biting taste of vinegar is a delightful addition to a variety of dishes. Vinegar heightens the flavor of soups and stews—and what would mayonnaise and salad dressings be without vinegar!

In the 1800s, raspberry vinegar, a twist of lemon and a tall tumbler of water was the country's favorite summer drink. Recently there has been a revival of interest in flavored vinegars. Available in all gourmet shops and even some supermarkets, these specialties carry a high price tag. There are delicious and interesting fruit vinegars that are uncomplicated and easy to produce in any home kitchen. Why not collect some attractive bottles and try your hand at making favorites for your pantry and some to give away as very personal and thoughtful gifts.

The following vinegar recipes call for the use of frozen fruit mainly because of its availability, and it seems a shame to use precious raspberries, when it is almost possible to bruise their fragile flesh with a look. Either fresh or frozen berries may be used in vinegars. If frozen, be sure to measure the fruit in the frozen form (see page 11).

Rosehips grow in prickly rose bushes in Alaska. This shrub plant produces large rose flowers. The orange-red berries, in season August and September, grow in Alaska, Canada, and the Rockies.

STERILIZING CONTAINERS

Vinegars will keep several months in sterilized containers without further processing or refrigeration. To sterilize, immerse container and lid completely in rapidly boiling water for 15–20 minutes. Invert onto clean towel to dry, then fill with vinegar and seal with hot sterilized lid or a new cork.

It's the Berries!

Blueberry Vinegar

PREPARATION: 10 MINUTES.
MAKES 1½ QUARTS.

4 cups blueberries; reserve 1 cup   4 tablespoons sugar
4 cups rice wine vinegar

Crush berries. Bring vinegar and sugar to a boil and pour over berries. Cover after cooling and put in sterile jar for 3–4 weeks and leave in a dark cool place. Shake or stir occasionally. After 4 weeks, strain, press essence down though sieve and discard fruit residue. Add reserved blueberries to vinegar as garnish.

The blueberry we know today is the work of Elizabeth C. White of New Jersey, who with several other women fruit growers, offered prizes locally for highbush blueberries bearing large fruits. She worked with a plant breeder and crossed many plants that she and her contestants had selected from the New Jersey Pine Barrens. The highbush or swamp blueberry is the one most widely distributed today.

Blueberry-Lemon Vinegar

PREPARATION: 10 MINUTES.
MAKES 5–5½ CUPS.

2 cups frozen blueberries   4 cups white wine vinegar
zest of 1 lemon, grated
½ cup frozen lemonade concentrate, undiluted

Put blueberries in nonmetal bowl. Crush with a wooden spoon. Add lemon zest and lemonade concentrate. In an enamel saucepan or glass pot, bring vinegar to a simmer. Pour over blueberry-lemon mixture. Cover with plastic wrap and put in dark place for 1 month. Strain through double cheesecloth. Squeeze out blueberry-lemon essence. Pour into sterile bottles. Place in dark place for 2 weeks before using.

Raspberry Vinegar

PREPARATION: 5 MINUTES.
MAKES 1½ QUARTS.

6 cups raspberries; reserve 3 cups   **3 cups rice wine vinegar**

Boil a 2-quart jar for 15 minutes to sterilize it. Divide raspberries. Thaw 3 cups. Freeze the other 3 cups. Crush the thawed berries and add vinegar. Prepare them for a water bath: put mixture in 2-quart jar in a deep pot of water and bring the water around the bottle to a boil. Reduce heat and simmer for 20 minutes. Cool vinegar, cover, and place in a dark place. Stir each day. After two weeks, thaw reserved raspberries. Crush. Strain vinegar and press original raspberries through a strainer. Discard residue. Pour vinegar onto new raspberries and repeat the water bath. Let vinegar "marry" in a dark place 2 more weeks. It is then ready for use or to pour in attractive bottles for a special gift.

RASPBERRY VINEGAR

Raspberry vinegar is perhaps the favorite of all the fruit vinegars. Its delicate, savory flavor makes this vinegar excel as the perfect mate to a delicate olive oil when dressing tender greens. It adds gentle zest to a sauté of scallops or chicken breasts, and it's a welcome splash on fresh fruit salads. Drizzled over fresh strawberries and raspberries, it heightens the berries' sun-kissed flavors.

Blackberries are known as brambleberries in England. Blackberries are one of the oldest fruits known. They grow in Asia, North America, Europe, and South Africa. Originally, when North America was settled, blackberries were scarce due to heavy forests. As the land was cleared, these berries spread. Cultivation began in 1825.

Raspberry-Ginger Vinegar

PREPARATION: 10 MINUTES.
MAKES 4 CUPS.

4 cups raspberries
3 cups white wine vinegar

⅓ cup sugar
1 gingerroot, grated

Crush raspberries with wooden spoon. Add vinegar and pour into sterile jar. Close jar tightly and put in a dark place for 3 weeks. After this time, sieve through double cheesecloth. Heat in an enamel or glass pot and add sugar. Cook on low flame until the sugar dissolves. Add grated ginger. Put in a sterile jar, cap, and leave in a dark place for 2 more weeks.

Blackberry Citrus Vinegar

PREPARATION: 10 MINUTES.
MAKES 1 QUART.

4 cups blackberries
lemon zest strips from 1 lemon
orange zest strips from 1 orange

½ cup sweet white wine
3½ cups white vinegar

Put blackberries in enamel or glass saucepan. Crush with wooden spoon. Add lemon and orange strips. Heat wine and white vinegar to just below a boil. Pour over berries. Stir. Cover with plastic wrap. Put in dark place for 3 weeks. Stir. Strain essence through 2 pieces of cheesecloth, discard fruit. Bottle in sterile jar and place liquid in a dark place so flavors "marry."

The black raspberry is the fruit of the Rubus plant. The succulent fleshy berry is red and deep purple and is grown mainly in Michigan, Oregon, New York, and Washington.

Strawberry Vinegar

PREPARATION: 10 MINUTES.
MAKES 5 CUPS.

2 cups strawberries
1 cup of champagne and 1 cup for later (optional)
2 cups white wine vinegar

8 whole black peppercorns, cracked
1½ teaspoons sugar

Mash strawberries. Heat the champagne, wine vinegar, peppercorns, and sugar together. Pour over strawberries in sterile jar. Cool, cover, and place in a dark place for 1 month. Stir occasionally. Press out strawberry flesh between double cheesecloth, discard the fruit. Add the second cup of champagne to the vinegar mixture. Stir to release the carbonation. Allow to rest in a dark place for 1 month.

Blueberry-Orange Vinegar

PREPARATION: 10 MINUTES.
MAKES 1 QUART.

2 cups blueberries
zest of 1 orange

4 cups white wine vinegar
⅓ cup sugar

Put blueberries and orange zest in a large pan. Bring vinegar and sugar to a boil and pour over berries. Cool and cover. Put in sterile jar. Steep for 2 days before using. Store in a cool place.

Cooking Tip. The best zest is tangerine zest. Use it instead of orange when available for a superior flavor. When tangerines are in season, peel the outside skin off with a carrot scraper, and dry in a low oven on a rack. Keep in a covered jar to preserve the essence.

Favorite Flavored Vinegar Combinations

- White wine vinegar with blueberries, rosemary, and orange rind
- Red wine vinegar with fresh blueberries
- Champagne vinegar with raspberry extract and fresh raspberries

Best Brands of Vinegar

Chicama Vineyards Cranberry Vinegar
    Made at Martha's Vineyard. This is truly a delicious, tart vinegar.

Paul Corcellet Raspberry Vinegar
    This vinegar has a rich raspberry flavor. Good as a drink, with water. Not overpowering.

Pommery Raspberry Vinegar
    Made since 1865. A very clear vinegar that is delicious poured over a baking apple.

SoReiclou White Wine Vinegar with three fruits
    A clear pink French vinegar made with raspberries, strawberries, and bilberries. A marvelous fruity flavor.

The Silver Palate Blueberry and Raspberry Vinegars
    Both blueberry and raspberry vinegars are fragrant but not overly sweet.

Suppliers of Berry Products

For special gifts, unusual ingredients, and berries from far away places, we've found these suppliers to be wonderful resources. We selected sources that fill orders rapidly, and ship them carefully. The merchandise is of a consistently high quality. The prices and addresses are current as of January, 1988.

Huckleberry Jam

This wild fruit is made into jam in Spokane, Washington. The only huckleberries used are those that grow in the rugged panhandle area of northern Idaho.

For the last two years, the terrain where the berries grow has been so rugged the berries are picked by retired loggers. The jam is made only during the four-month berry season and amazingly each berry in the jam is whole. The jam is tart, mild, and spicy. A 12-ounce jar is $6.00. A **free** brochure is available from: **Wilds of Idaho, 1308 West Boone, Spokane, WA 99201. 509-326-0197**

Honey

Ever tasted raspberry or blueberry honey? They are delicious! A **free** brochure is available from: **R. B. Swan & Son, 25 Prospect Street, Brewer, ME 04412. 207-989-3622**

Currant Preserves

An island maritime climate similar to that of England, with warm days and cool nights, produces intensely flavorful berries for currant preserves. For a **free** brochure send to: **The Maury Island Farming Co., Route 3, Box 238, Vashon, WA 98020. 206-463-9659**

Cranberry Confections

The Cranberry Sweets Company makes 27 kinds of cranberry jellies. These are deep red sparkling sugar-coated jellies. Tangy, chewy, and delicious they are covered with a layer of granular sugar. There are no preservatives or artificial flavors used in these candies. Send for a **free** list of assortment and prices: **Cranberry Sweets Company, P.O. Box 501, Bandon, OR 97411. 503–347-2526**

More Fruit, Less Sugar

Linn's Fruit Bin produces an almost sugarless product. Each preserve is handmade in small batches at a family farm. Available are: olallieberry, red raspberry, raspberry-rhubarb, kiwifruit, and peach-blueberry preserves. For a **free** price list and catalog send to: **Linn's Fruit Bin, RR 1, Box 600, Cambria, CA 93428. 805-927-1499**

Chocolate

Love chocolate? How about chocolate and berries? Pine Mountain offers: apple-cranberry chocolates, huckleberry cordials, Montana huckleberry chocolate assortment, Montana huckleberry

It's the Berries!

chocolates, huckleberry cream chocolates, and huckleberry-walnut stix. A **free** mail order catalog is available from: **Pine Mountain Chocolates P.O. Box 2091, Missoula, MT 59806. 406-728-6916**

Fruit Vinegars

On Martha's Vineyard there is a winery that also specializes in making excellent full-flavored fruit vinegars. The fruits used are farm grown, and the final product is both delicious and incredibly clear, as it is steeped in oak barrels for months. For a **free** price list write to: **Chicama Vineyards, Stoney Hill Road, West Tisbury, MA 02575. 617-693-0309**

Cranberry Catsup

A sophisticated condiment whose producers go to New Jersey each year to get the finest cranberries grown for flavor and color. Delicious with poultry! **Free** flyer available from: **Homespun, Inc. 3205-C Sutton Place N.W., Washington, DC 20016. 202-244-7712**

Cranberry Chutney

If you want a chutney that is superior in taste and versatility, send for Steele's. Once you taste it you will always want to have a supply handy to accompany chicken, turkey, lamb, or pork. Also, a delightful gift! Call or write: **C. Steele & Company, 909 East Camelback Road, Phoenix, AZ 85014. 602-994-4180 (Grocery Dept.)**

Raspberry Splendors

Sophisticated raspberry sauces (decadent chocolate), fruity jam, lovely raspberry vinegar, and a terrific cookbook—all from the

Thomson family's farm in Duluth, Minnesota. Write for a **free** mail order catalog from: **Thomson Berry Farms, 525 Lake Avenue South, Duluth, MN 55802. 218-722-2529**

Industry Sources

Sources of Information

Hammonton Blueberry
  Exchange
548 Pleasant Mills Road
Hammonton, NJ 08037
609-561-3661

Michigan Blueberry Growers'
  Association
P.O. Drawer B
Grand Junction, MI 49056
616-434-6791

North American Blueberry
  Council
P.O. Box 166
Marmora, NJ 08223
609-399-1559

Ocean Spray Cranberries
  Incorporated
Fresh Cranberry Division
Water Street
Plymouth, MA 02360
617-747-1000

California Kiwifruit
  Commission
1540 River Park Drive
Suite 120
Sacramento, CA 95816
916-929-5314

New Zealand Kiwifruit
  Authority
1750 Montgomery Street
San Francisco, CA 94111-1011
415-788-4353

California Strawberry Advisory
  Board
P.O. Box 269
Watsonville, CA 95077
408-724-1301

General Information

United Fresh Fruit &
  Vegetable Association
P.O. Box 1417 East 35
N. Washington & Madison Aves.
Alexandria, VA 22314
703-836-3410

Frieda's Finest Produce
  Specialities, Inc.
P.O. Box 58488
Los Angeles, CA 90028
213-627-2981

Bibliography

Alaska Wild Berry Guide and Cookbook, editors et al. *Alaska Magazine,* Anchorage, AK: Alaska Northwest Publishing Company, 1982. *Complete guide to a wide variety of berries that grow in Alaska and some Northwestern states with descriptions, photos, growing seasons and some recipes.*

Berried Treasures, Elaine Jauman. Osseo, MN: Kitchen Treasures Publishing, 1982. *Recipes for most commonly grown berries.*

Berries, Raspberries & Black, Pownal, VT: Garden Way Publishing Bulletin A-33, 1979. *Growing and knowing raspberries.*

The Berry Book, Robert Henrickson. Garden City, NY: Doubleday, 1981. *History, growing information, with select traditional recipes for American berries.*

The Berry Cookbook, Kyle D. Fulwiler. Seattle, WA: Pacific Search Press, 1985. *Handling, cooking common berries.*

Berry Cooking, Gertrude Mann. London, England: Andre Deutsch Ltd., 1954. *British berry recipes and classic serving ideas.*

Better Homes and Gardens Five Seasons Cranberry Cookbook, editors of *Better Homes and Gardens Magazine*. Des Moines, IA: Meredith Publishing Co., 1971. *Recipes for cranberries—fresh, frozen, and canned.*

The Blueberry Connection, Beatrice Ross Buszek. Halifax, Nova Scotia: Nimbus Publishing Ltd., 1977. (Distributed by Yankee Books, Dublin, NH). *Basic handling, information, and recipes.*

The Complete Strawberry, Strafford Whiteaker. Crown, NY: 1985. *A tribute to the strawberry—the strawberry through history, in literature, art, and politics. Some growing information and select recipes. Beautiful reproductions of old prints.*

The Cranberry Connection, Beatrice Ross Buszek. Halifax, Nova Scotia: Nimbus Publishing Ltd., 1977. (Distributed by Yankee Books, Dublin, NH). *Basic handling information, and recipes.*

Growing and Cooking Berries, Mary W. Corning. Dublin, NH: Yankee Books, 1980. *Focuses on common berry varieties.*

Grow the Best Blueberries, Pownal, VT: Garden Way Publishing Bulletin A-89, 1982. *Just that.*

Grow the Best Strawberries, Pownal, VT: Garden Way Publishing Bulletin A-1, 1977. *Just that.*

Mad About Raspberries and Strawberries, Jacqueline Heriteau, Putnam, NY: Pedigree Books, 1984. *Information and recipes.*

More Berried Treasures, Elaine Jauman. Osseo, MN: Kitchen Treasures Publishing, 1983. *More recipes.*

Simply Strawberries, Sara Pitzer. Pownal, VT: Garden Way Publishing, 1985. *Information and recipes to celebrate strawberries.*

The Strawberry Connection, Beatrice Ross Buszek. Halifax, Nova Scotia: Nimbus Publishing Ltd., 1977. (Distributed by Yankee Books, Dublin, NH). *Recipes for strawberries.*

Index

It's the Berries!